Hesitant Wolf & Scrupulous Fox

Hesitant Wolf & Scrupulous Fox:

Fables Selected from World Literature

EDITED AND WITH AN INTRODUCTION
by Karen Kennerly

SCHOCKEN BOOKS · NEW YORK

First published by Schocken Books 1983
10 9 8 7 6 5 4 3 2 1   83 84 85 86
Copyright © 1973 by Karen Kennerly
All rights reserved
Published by agreement with Random House, Inc.

Library of Congress Cataloging in Publication Data
Main entry under title:
Hesitant wolf & scrupulous fox.
Reprint. Originally published: 1st ed. New York: Random House, 1973.
Includes index.
SUMMARY: Over 150 fables selected from 5,000 years of literature.
I. Fables.   [I. Fables]   I. Kennerly, Karen.
II. Title: Hesitant wolf and scrupulous fox.
[PN982.K4 1982]   398.2'452   82–3328   AACR2

Designed by Antonina Krass
Manufactured in the United States of America
ISBN 0–8052–0717–1

Grateful acknowledgment is made to the following for permission to re-print previously published material:

The Balkin Agency: For "Coyote and Junco" ("At Gourd-Patch Rise Old Lady Junco Had Her Home and Coyote") from *Finding the Center: Narrative Poetry of the Zuni Indians*, translated by Dennis Tedlock. Copyright © 1972 by Dennis Tedlock; Copyright © 1978 by University of Nebraska Press.

A. S. Barnes, San Diego, California: For adaptations of "The Snail and the Mirror" and "The Black Marten" from *Aesop Without Morals*, translated by Lloyd W. Daley. Published by Thomas Yoseloff.

A. S. Barnes, San Diego, California, and UNESCO: For "Ape, Glow-Worm, and Bird" from *The Panchatantra*, translated by Franklin Edgerton. English translation from the Sanskrit. © UNESCO 1965.

Jonathan Cape Ltd. and the Estate of Pablo Neruda: For "Fable of the Mermaid and the Drunks" from *We Are Many* by Pablo Neruda, translated by Alistair Reid.

Columbia University Press: For "The Sea-Bird" (page 194) and "Chuang Chou Hunting" (pages 218–219) from *The Complete Works of Chuang Tzu* (1968), translated by Burton Watson. For "Keeper of the Royal Hat" (page 32) and "The Rich Man of Sung" (page 77) from *Han Fei Tzu: Basic Writings* (1964), translated by Burton Watson. For "Chüang Shu-liang in the Moonlight" (pages 134–135) from *Hsün-Tzu: Basic Writings* (1963) translated by Burton Watson. For "Beans and Husks" (page 62) from *Essays in Idleness* (1967), Kenkō, translated by Donald Keene.

J. M. Dent and Sons Ltd.: For "A Country Mouse and a Town Mouse" from *The Collected Works of Horace* by Horace, translated by Lord Dunsany and Michael Oakley. Everyman's Library Series.

Doubleday & Company, Inc. and Faber and Faber Ltd.: For "The Lady and

Quarterly Review of Literature and Michael Hamburger: For the translations of "Zeus and the Horse" and "Story of the Old Wolf" by G. E. Lessing. First appeared in *Quarterly Review of Literature*, Vol. XVIII, No. 1–2, 1972.

William Saroyan: For "How the Pompous Remark of the Turtle Spoiled the Last Moments of the Lion," "How the Hair of Woman Is Long, the Understanding Short, and What a Ghastly Lack of Appreciation There Is in Them for Genius" from *Saroyan's Fables*. Copyright 1941 by William Saroyan. (Harcourt Brace Jovanovich, Inc.)

Schocken Books, Inc.: For "A Little Fable" from *The Great Wall of China* by Franz Kafka. Copyright © 1946 by Schocken Books, Inc.

Simon & Schuster, a Division of Gulf & Western Corporation, and Jonathan Cape Ltd.: For "Randolf's Party" from *In His Own Write* by John Lennon. Copyright © 1964 by John Lennon.

Teachers & Writers Collaborative: For "The Fox and the Grapes" by Donald Gear.

Mrs. James Thurber: For "The Fox and the Crow" and "Variations on the Theme" from *Fables for Our Time* by James Thurber. Copyright 1940 by James Thurber, copyright © 1968 by Helen Thurber. Published by Harper & Row, Publishers, Inc. Both originally appeared in *The New Yorker*.

The University of Chicago Press: For "The Donkey and the Jackel," "The Frogs That Rode Snakeback," "Butter-Blinded Brahman," "The Blue Jackal," "Mice That Ate Iron," and "Poor Blossom" from *The Panchatantra*, translated by Arthur W. Ryder. Copyright © 1956 by The University of Chicago.

The University of Michigan Press: For "The Hawk and the Nightingale" from *Works and Days*, by Hesiod, translated by Richmond Lattimore. Copyright © 1959 by The University of Michigan.

The University Press of Virginia: For "The Fox and the Grapes," "Mountain in Labor," and "The Frog Jealous of the Ox" from *The Best Fables of La Fontaine*, translated by Francis Duke.

Viking Penguin Inc. and The Society of Authors as the literary representative of the Estate of James Joyce: For "The Mookse and the Gripes" from *Finnegans Wake* by James Joyce. Copyright © 1939 by James Joyce; copyright renewed 1967 by George Joyce and Lucia Joyce.

FOR JERRY

Foreword

A folklorist to whom I described the contents of this book politely scorned the possibility of linking oral and written works with the common definition "fable." And it wouldn't surprise me if an Aesopian scholar questioned the juxtaposition of a fable by Babrius and a story by John Lennon.

The main reason I brought these particular fables together is to free the fable from constrictions of genre and of external form, and to focus on the internal properties of fables that make them distinct from folk tales, satires, myths, parables. Exacting as these criteria must be, fables are nevertheless universal since they are informed by attitudes toward human behavior; literary style is their encasement. This is something La Fontaine was aware of when he apologized for the ornamentation of his fables which, he wrote, made them less effective than more stark renditions by the Greeks. On the other end of the spectrum, a similar tension is felt in a fable extracted from mythology or from folklore. Thus one might say that fables are a loose analogue to the Structuralist concept of a "universal grammar" which underlies all literature.

In the first part of the book, the fables are grouped according to various themes. No fable should be considered bound to its category, which is a point I hoped to make clear by leaving those in the second part unburdened by divisions. The book does not attempt to be comprehensive, but the scope of fables is as broad as I could make it. Some literatures—Norwegian is one—I did not have access to because I don't know the language and wasn't fortunate enough to encounter someone who did. Others, like Japanese, have produced virtually no fables. The same is true of Gaelic literature, where a fascination with myth and tragedy took such a strong hold of its sensibility that it seems to have excluded more pragmatic, "fabulous" tales. Many of the West African stories which are thought to be fables because they contain fable motifs are—in my opinion—ultimately folk tales and not fables as such. If my concept of what *is* a fable appears to be unnecessarily precise—some may even call it rigid—it is not because I deny their humor and whimsy, but because their very simplicity defines them as a unique form in literature.

K.K.

Acknowledgments

My thanks are due to the following people who translated, adapted or wrote fables specifically for this collection: Jerome Charyn, Robert Fitzgerald, Michael Hamburger, Richard Howard, Leonard Jenkin, Martin Lopez-Morillas, Mark Mirsky, and Ivan Morris. I am particularly indebted to Herbert Kohl who, as director of the Teachers and Writers Collaborative in 1968, asked me to research fables for a curriculum unit and subsequently encouraged the sort of thinking about fables that led to the inception of this book. The predictable list of favorable adjectives for friends who helped in various ways apply to the following: Cordelia Jason, Antonina Krass, John J. Simon, Aaron Asher, Donald Barthelme, Jerome Charyn, Donald Hutter, Ivan Morris, Jane Seitz, and the librarians at the British Museum.

 Contents

3. Fables which are peopled by those who never will perceive the foolishness of their actions

4. Fables which make social and political statements

5. Variant plays on the same fables

6. Fables juxtaposed to display various aspects of fabulous animals

7. Various oral and literary modes which narrate fables

8. Fables couched in other literary forms

PART TWO

"Fables are a succession of changes."

List of Illustrations

Hesitant Wolf & Scrupulous Fox

Introduction

A snail falls in love with a mirror. He crawls onto its surface, caresses, licks, until the mirror loses all capacity to reflect. The teller of the tale calls in an observant monkey to instruct us: Those who allow themselves to be thus embraced, deserve the result. Only after the reader has put the fable down does he know that the *fabulist* has been summoning him to his own narcissism. If we learn from the monkey it is because we were seduced by the snail, who in an excess of love has rendered the adored object imperceptible. The monkey's admonition makes us attentive now to the mirror: Needful of praise, it will risk that which is most praiseworthy—its shine. We nurse our foibles—a fact camouflaged by the vanity of accomplishment. So, like children, we delight in having them exposed for us—we delight in the dependable finger of authority, wagging, wagging consequences. Once presented with boundaries of wisdom and rational behavior we are assured that we may be foolish all over again.

Licensed for narcissism, knowing at some level—although few literatures remind us and life does everything to conceal it—that vanity and narcissism are quite different, the former an unknowing of the latter, we are primed to take the roughest blows the fabulist offers. He deals with human behavior untinted by passion and unpalliated by aspiration. Cowardliness, boasting, canniness, uncanniness, equivocation, morality, hope—nothing is spared. Fables are amoral and unredemptive. They are innocent of morality. Happily ever after belongs to the fairy tale, never to the fable. God belongs to the parable. Fables may be cruel, but in their denial of original sin they are also incapable of damning: we always "go free."

Still, the narrative is one of condemnation. Two actors, or camps, are introduced in states of neutrality. They encounter, horns lock, and they cannot disengage until an inevitable series of moves declares a winner and a loser. (Or two losers, in which case *we* are given the victory.) A judgment has been made, within the story. But at the core, fable is paradox because victory is as temporary in its complexion as it is definitive in its narration. The fox, taunting the crow about his inability to sing, gets him to open his beak in protest and drop the cheese. Munching, content, the fox trots off. But when he leaps for grapes and fails, he slinks away muttering something about sourness.

The effectiveness of this is that one need not look to the corpus of fables to find it. It is there in the exquisitely balanced disinterest the fabulist has for trickster and tricked alike. The neutrality of the actors' entrance is possible because they have no history. Their lack of a sense of their own history is a kind of solipsism which relieves us of the burden of caring. Only their acts are important. Without care, there can be no bias. Admiration for the brute and sympathy for the timid are of equal fascination. Fables embody the demands Schiller made of comedy: that it be "Identical with man's highest aspirations, namely to be free of passion, to be able to look into and about himself calmly and perspicaciously, to discover everywhere more choice than fate, and to laugh at the incongruity, rather than deplore the infamy of things."

Where comedy uses caricature to display aspects of

behavior, fables employ reduction, which also defines their literary form. The snake *is* cleverness provoked by greed. The frogs *are* gullibility triggered by vanity. And a fable can only be about the interaction between snake and frog, each an obverse of the other. We read a tale about two or three characters of whom we know everything: with equal clarity we are also reading of our several selves and are momentarily confronted with a simple story raised to its square. Then the burlesque comes into focus. Fabled characters attach themselves like nagging shadows. We parallel one another. But the process of the fable is one of self-distillation. We are left not with parallels but essences of human behavior—no longer theirs exclusively nor ours particularly. The elegant deer takes the beauty of her spotted fawns for granted, until the fox, observing his own brood, asks the deer how she made them so lovely. Sudden vanity provokes a vicious answer: The sparks of a cedarwood fire branded them prettily, that's why they are spotted. The anxious fox tucks his children under a bed of hot ashes; but when he removes them, they are charred and dead. We are at once the deer with our own natural gift, and the fox who feels inferior in the presence of another's gift. When confronted, we have the need to ascribe that gift to our creative endeavors. We will also go to desperate measures to graft on to ourselves the talents of others. Hence all roles are interchangeable in fables. Such a fluidity is not possible in satire or allegory, which freeze their forms at the point of parallel. What is masked as fate is in fact choice, but a choice stripped of any pretense of intellectual control. The fable bluntly informs us that the moment of choosing slips beyond the forethought that initiated it. Hence, true rational behavior lies somewhere between animal instinct and the rationalized perception we hold of our most sober actions.

Wolf, the bully, Bestiary creature of fang and paw, unbeautiful and all too fathomable, is most unloved in the pantheon of animals. He is also the creature most like us. Released from history, we cannot prejudge him as we could when he was an iconographic object. We observe him prepare his impetuous attacks and realize his greed is obsessive. Always prowling, he seems acutely uncomfortable when alone. His paranoid fear that others do not value his intelligence is most frequently his undoing. When he overhears a mother threaten to throw her crying child to the wolves, he forgets about the barnyard animals he could easily make off with—a child is much finer stuff. He waits, docile, expectant by the door. The child cries louder and the mother softens: "Don't cry, we'll kill him if he comes." Instead of leaving like the sensible fox, he sulks, hurt and indignant. Contradictions! Do they take me for an idiot? That moment of hesitation may be his life. Out of phase with himself, he is defeated alternately by hubris and naïveté.

Like all fabulous actors, the wolf is true to his archetype. He affects greed, tyranny, brute power unmodulated by canniness. But these attitudes can be personified by others: fox/jackal, lion/cat, bear/lion. Since the fabulist is interested not in abstractions but in essences, a new and constant archetype draws its definition. Wolf becomes the irreconcilability between instinct and rational thought. He is our self-dramatization of the Fall. We wallow in

Expulsion. Convinced that we are totally *un*natural, we inflate pain into suffering, equate solitude with tragedy.

In fact, we are not as "fallen" as we like to think, Fox stands to correct Wolf. Most unconscious of animals, only fox, the Trickster, can play dead to catch his prey— and never die. For him winning or losing does not sing of the dread of life-or-death. He is not burdened by self-identity. Awareness is synonymous with spontaneous action. Unacquainted with terror or vanity, he is in a position of supreme self-confidence. All events, be they engaging wolf in a well-bucket dip that leaves wolf stranded with moon-cheese, or scurrying from hunters, have the same weight for him: they free him from over-reaction. When he does lose, it is in a sensible game. Innocent of law, he is essentially anarchical, and this is the source of his power. Fox stands immovably central amidst the disorder he creates. It is not curious, then, that the animal whose sense of self is most amorphous is also the one most sharply outlined for other fabulous actors. And for us. His physical attributes are easy to grasp, nicely comprehensible: medium-sized, red coat, a loose-jointed gait. He is adorable when behaving himself, but never poignant. Adorable also when he is wicked, since he cannot be vicious. His effect is as predictable as his games are inscrutable.

The neutrality of Trickster, of fox, makes it nearly impossible for us to assume an attitude about him. Polar to wolf, fox is the fusion of instinct and rational behavior. He is that self we are least intuitive about and resist admitting: it undermines our singular gift of brooding. Wolf stands at our entrance into the fable; Fox runs through its landscape touching all points where fabled creatures meet.

Most animals have found their way into fables—including man. Humans can be depersonalized just as animals are sheared of their mythic archetypes. If animals are given the ability to speak without implications of humanness, man's intercourse with the animal kingdom does not suggest saintliness. Rather, the condition of animals suffuses man, which is why one often forgets that the latter figures in fables at all. His distinction is his passivity, his attribute, that-which-must-be-taught, simply. He is foil to serpent, but serpent as teacher, not tempter. The farmer offers the snake a dish of milk in pleasant whimsy; it is the snake's gold coin which actualizes their friendship. And even after the farmer's son has clipped off the snake's tail, and the snake has coiled round and killed him, even then the farmer carries the ritual milk to the snake. Unapproachable now inside his hole, the snake teaches the farmer about bitterness without blame. And ends their friendship. The farmer turns back, a little wiser but not destroyed.

The animal world is an obvious terrain for fables. A connected series of designs cannot be attributed to its inhabitants. They are incapable—from our perspective—of knowing the consequences of their actions until after these have been experienced. The unlandscaped nature and subterranean cities in which they dwell do not invite a fixing of place, which would truncate the omnipresence of fabled truth. We are given only the necessary signposts: cave, pasture, hole, tree hollow, nest, kitchen door. Their gift of speech works also as "sign" rather than miracle, because their articulated plottings direct them toward their natural goals. Fox sniffs for hens, Serpent for eagle's eggs. Our delight in incongruities is sprung open when we are told that "The monkey was thinking to himself one day . . ." And the fabulist does work through incongruity. Suspension of disbelief is not his mode.

Disparities are spread about us in a polite circle. But like little magnets they tug toward one another, passing through us, charging us. We stand on a spot equidistant from our two responses to animals—to fables. We regard their harmony wistfully, even with awe. They are also base—lovable mascots, valuable for our subsistence, but ultimately ours to use and to dispose of. These creatures who reside on the edges of peripheral vision now are placed, through a subtle manipulation of incongruities, in front of us. Because the periphery has been left void, they fill the space of our own mirrors. Incongruity also plays the narrative against the literature. The past tense (directly or implicitly) gives us a story that happened once and once only. "The birds met to choose more kings . . ." Yet by implication we know that the tale itself is a metaphor for something that has happened before and will happen again. Always spilling over its form, the fable is the perfect art of the miniaturist.

Part One

Cynical fables, in which we
are doomed no matter how exemplary our behavior may be

A Little Fable

Alas, said the mouse, "the world is growing smaller every day. At the beginning it was so big that I was afraid, I kept running and running, and I was glad when at last I saw walls far away to the right and left, but these long walls have narrowed so quickly that I am in the last chamber already, and there in the corner stands the trap that I must run into." "You only need to change your direction," said the cat, and ate it up.

—FRANZ KAFKA
translated by Willa and Edwin Muir

The Sea-Bird

Haven't you heard this story? Once a sea bird alighted in the suburbs of the Lu capital. The marquis of Lu escorted it to the ancestral temple, where he entertained it, performing the Nine Shao music for it to listen to and presenting it with the meat of the T'ai-lao sacrifice to feast on. But the bird only looked dazed and forlorn, refusing to eat a single slice of meat or drink a cup of wine, and in three days it was dead.

—CHUANG TZU
translated by Burton Watson

🐍The Snake and the Shepherd

O nce upon a time there was a shepherd, and while he was milking his sheep he saw a snake crawling out of its hole and going about among his sheep. When the shepherd saw it, he poured some milk in a pot for the snake, and the snake drank it. The day after he poured some milk in the pot again, he put it near the snake's hole, and said: "My dear little snake, come out to drink some nice sweet milk," and the snake came out and drank it. When the shepherd went to get the pot he found a gold coin beside it, and he was very glad. At noon he put the pot of milk by its hole again and it came out and drank it, and it left another coin for him. And in the evening he poured some milk in the pot again, and he called it, and the snake came out and drank the milk. So the snake and the shepherd made friends, and he took some milk for the snake three times a day, and it left three gold coins for him each day till the shepherd got very rich and decided to go to the Holy Grave. He told his wife to give the milk to the snake every morning at dawn, every noon and every evening. Then he set out.

The shepherd's wife gave the snake its milk every day. The shepherd had also a little boy about five or six years old, and one day the boy was walking around among the sheep petting them and playing with them, but the snake was around too, crawling here and there. The boy did not see it and stepped on its tail, and the boy's pigskin shoes that had nails sticking out of their soles, cut off the snake's tail. Then the snake, hurt as it was, turned its head and bit the boy, and the boy was poisoned and died. And after the boy had died they buried him. At noon they put the pot of milk by the snake's hole, but the snake did not come out to drink it. In the evening they went to pour some more milk in the pot, but they saw that the milk they had poured at noon had not been drunk. So they did not put the pot of milk there any more, and the snake did not appear to crawl about in the fold any longer.

Six months went by; the shepherd came back from the Holy Grave and as he did not see his child, he asked his wife: "Where's our boy?" "Our boy was bitten by the snake and died," said his wife. The shepherd did not say anything, he only poured some milk in the pot and he went to put it by the snake's hole and said to the snake: "My dear little snake, come out to drink some nice sweet milk!" But the snake shouted from inside: "Alas! Shepherd! As long as you remember your dead boy and I turn my head and see my tail cut off, what kind of friendship can exist between us?" So the friendship between the shepherd and the snake was broken.

—GREECE

contemporary oral version of Aesop translated by Georgios A. Megas

The Hawk and the Nightingale

Now I will tell you a fable for the barons;
    they understand it.
That is what the hawk said when he had caught
    a nightingale
with spangled neck in his claws and carried her
    high among the clouds.
She, spitted on the clawhooks, was wailing pitifully,
but the hawk, in his masterful manner,
    gave her an answer:
"What is the matter with you? Why scream?
    Your master has you.
You shall go wherever I take you,
    for all your singing.
If I like, I can let you go. If I like,
    I can eat you for dinner.
He is a fool who tries to match his strength
    with the stronger.
He will lose his battle, and with the shame
    will be hurt also."
So spoke the hawk, the bird who flies so fast
    on his long wings.

—HESIOD

translated by Richmond Lattimore

🌸Poor Blossom

God Indra once had a parrot named Blossom. He enjoyed supreme beauty, loveliness, and various graces, while his intelligence was not blunted by his extensive scientific attainments.

One day he was resting on the palm of great Indra's hand, his body thrilling with delight at that contact, and was reciting a variety of authoritative formulas, when he caught sight of Yama, lord of death, who had come to pay his respects at the time appointed. Seeing the god, the parrot edged away. And all the thronging immortals asked him: "Why did you move away, sir, upon beholding that personage?" "But," said the parrot, "he brings harm to all living creatures. Why not move away from him?"

Upon hearing this, they all desired to calm his fears, so said to Yama: "As a favor to us, you must please not kill this parrot." And Yama replied: "I do not know about that. It is Time who determines these matters."

They therefore took Blossom with them, paid a visit to Time, and made the same request. To which Time replied: "It is Death who is posted in these affairs. Pray speak to him."

But when they did so, the parrot died at the mere sight of Death. And they were all distressed at seeing the occurrence, so that they said to Yama: "What does this mean?" And Yama said: "It was simply fated that he should die at the mere sight of Death." With this reply they went back to heaven.

—from *The Panchatantra*
translated by Arthur W. Ryder

The Obedient Dog

A dog barked all night because of thieves.
  His sleepless master beat him black and blue.
On the next night the dog slept; thieves came.
And the silent dog was beaten again.

—IGNACY KRASICKI

adapted by Karen Kennerly from the
translation by Jerzy Peterkiewicz and
Burns Singer

A Fox and a Dragon

As a *Fox* was Earthing Himself, he Digg'd so Deep, 'till at last he came to a *Dragon's Den*, where he found a Prodigious Mass of Hidden Treasure. He made his Excuse for his Intrusion, and Begg'd the Dragon's leave but to Ask him One Question. Pray (says he) where's the Pleasure or the Profit of Spending all your Days in a Hole thus, without either Light or Sleep? Why 'tis me *Fate*, says the *Dragon*, and there's no more to be said. Here's a Monstrous Hord, says the *Fox*, and I cannot find that you either Give or Use One Peny out of all this store. 'Tis a Misery, says the other, that I am Doom'd to, and there's no Avoiding it. Why then says the Fox, He that's Born under Your Stars is certainly the most Wretched of Creatures.

—ROGER L'ESTRANGE

Keeper of the Royal Hat

O nce in the past Marquis Chao of Han got drunk and fell asleep. The Keeper of the Royal Hat, seeing that the Marquis was cold, laid a robe over him. When the Marquis awoke, he was pleased and asked his attendants, "Who covered me with a robe?" "The Keeper of the Hat," they replied. The Marquis thereupon punished both the Keeper of the Royal Hat and the Keeper of the Royal Robe. He punished the Keeper of the Robe for failing to do his duty, and the Keeper of the Hat for overstepping his office.

—HAN FEI TZU
translated by Burton Watson

Randolf's Party

It was Chrisbus time but Randolph was alone. Where were all his good pals, Bernie, Dave, Nicky, Alice, Beddy, Freba, Viggy, Nigel, Alfred, Clive, Stan, Frenk, Tom, Harry, George, Harold? Where were they on this day? Randolf looged saggly at his only Chrispbut cart from his dad who did not live there.

"I can't understan this being so aloneley on the one day of the year when one would surely spect a pal or two?" thought Rangolf. Hanyway hecarried on putting ub the desicrations and muzzle toe. All of a surgeon there was amerry timble on the door. Who but who could be a knocking on my door? He opened it and there standing there who? but only his pals. Bernie, Dave, Nicky, Alice, Beddy, Freba, Viggy, Nigel, Alfred, Clive, Stan, Frenk, Tom, Harry, George, Harolb weren't they?

Come on in old pals buddys and mates. With a big griff on his face Randoff welcombed them. In they came jorking and labbing shoubing "Haddy Grimmble, Randoob." and other hearty, and then they all jumbed on him and did smite him with mighty blows about his head crying, "We never liked you all the years we've known you. You were never raelly one of us you know, soft head."

They killed him you know, at least he didn't *die* alone did he? Merry Chrustchove, Randolf old pal buddy.

—John Lennon

The Nut and the Campanile

A Nut found itself carried by a Crow to the top of a tall Campanile, and by falling into a crevice succeeded in escaping its dread fate. It then besought the Wall to shelter it; appealing to it by the grace of God, and praising its height, and the beauty and noble tone of its bells.

"Alas," it went on, "as I have not been able to drop beneath the green branches of my old Father and to lie in the fallow earth covered by his fallen leaves, do you, at least, not abandon me. When I found myself in the beak of the cruel Crow I made a vow, that if I escaped I would end my life in a little hole."

At these words, the Wall, moved with compassion, was content to shelter the Nut in the spot where it had fallen. Within a short time, the Nut burst open: its roots reached in between the crevices of the stones and began to push them apart; its shoots pressed up toward the sky. They soon rose above the building, and as the twisted roots grew thicker they began to thrust the walls apart and force the Ancient stones from their old places.

Then the Wall, too late and in vain, bewailed the cause of its destruction, and in a short time it fell in ruin.

—LEONARDO DA VINCI

Sick Kite and Her Mother

Pray *Mother* (says a sick Kite) Give over these Idle Lamentations, and let Me rather have your Prayers. Alas! my Child (says the Dam) which of the Gods shall I go to, for a Wretch that has Robb'd All their Altars?

—ROGER L'ESTRANGE

Fables of gentle warning:
Instruction suffices as due
punishment

Zeus and the Horse

Father of beasts and men," said the horse, prancing up to the throne of Zeus, "they call me one of the most handsome of all the creatures that grace this world, and my self-love urges me to believe them. But, all the same, might there not be this or that feature that could bear improvement?"

"What feature are you thinking of, then? Speak your mind. I am open to correction," said the kind god, and smiled.

"Perhaps," the horse continued, "I could be faster if my legs were longer and slimmer; a lithe swan's neck would do me no harm; a broader chest would add to my strength; and since you made it my business to carry your darling, man, you might have provided me with the saddle which the beneficent rider has to place on my back."

"Very well," Zeus replied, "just give me a moment. . . ." Grave-faced now, Zeus spoke the word of creation. The dust was quickened, organized matter combined; and before the throne there stood—the ugly c a m e l.

The horse saw it, shuddered and trembled with horrified disgust.

"Here are longer and slimmer legs," said Zeus; "here is a lithe swan's neck; here is a broader chest; here is your built-in saddle! Is that what you wanted, horse? To be transformed into that?"

The horse continued to tremble.

"Take yourself off," Zeus went on; "corrected without being punished—this time. Yet to remind you of your overreaching now and then, making you sorry for it, let this new creature also live on"—Zeus cast a preserving glance at the c a m e l—"and never shall the horse catch sight of you without a shudder."

—GOTTHOLD EPHRAIM LESSING
translated by Michael Hamburger

The Story of
the Hungry Elephant

Once there lived an Elephant, and he said to himself, "I am very hungry." He went along a path in the forest, and came to a bamboo-palm standing in a swamp. Roughly he tore down the palm; he saw a tender bud held in one of its leaves. But as he took the bud from the leaf, it fell into the water. He hunted and hunted, yet could not find it because he had riled up the water and it blinded his eyes. Then a frog spoke and said, "Listen!" The Elephant did not hear, thrashing the water hard with his trunk. The frog spoke again: "Listen!" The Elephant heard this time, and stood perfectly still, curious. Thereupon the water became clear so that he found the palm-bud and ate it.

—BULU   (*Kamerun, West Africa*)

The Rose

All other flowers around me also wither and die; and yet they call *me* the fading, the quick-fading Rose. Unthankful men! Do I not make my short existence agreeable enough for you? Yes, even after my death I prepare for you a remembrance—sweet odors, medicines and salves, potent with refreshment. Still, I always hear you say, and sing, 'Ah, the fading, the quick-fading Rose!' "

Thus complained the queen of flowers upon her throne, perhaps already in the first perception of her sinking beauty. An attendant maiden heard her and spoke: "Don't be angry at us, lovely one; call not unthankfulness that which is great love. We see all flowers around us die, and accept it as their fate; but it is you, their queen that we desire and thus hold worthy of immortality. And when we are disappointed, allow us grievances—we are also lamenting ourselves. The beauty, youth and joy in our lives we compare to you. And when we, like you, let our blossoms fall away, then do we sing, 'Ah, the fading, the quick-fading Rose!' "

—JOHANN GOTTFRIED VON HERDER

The Lion and the Mouse

A lion caught a mouse and was about to eat him. The little house-bred thief, now close to death, faintly muttering begged for life with words like these: "It's well for you to hunt down stags and horned bulls, and with their flesh make fat your belly. A mouse is not meal enough for you to taste with the edges of your lips. Come —spare me. Perhaps some day, though small, I shall repay this favor." The beast laughed and let his suppliant live. But before long he himself fell in with youthful lovers of the chase, and was taken captive in their net, made helpless, and bound fast. The mouse ran forth unnoticed from his hole, and, gnawing the sturdy rope with his tiny teeth, set the lion free. By saving thus in turn the lion's life, he made a recompense well worth the gift of life that he'd received.

—BABRIUS

translated by Ben Edwin Perry

Cock in His Litter

A cock had some cats as his litter-bearers. As he thus palanquined in sprawling languor, a fox stepped up beside him and said: "I advise you to watch out for treachery; if you looked closely into the faces of those bearers, you might conclude that they are not porters with a load, but hunters bringing home their booty."

—AESOP   (*Perotti's Index*)

adapted from Ben Edwin Perry's translation
by Karen Kennerly

Fable of the Man and of the Lyon

Men ought not to byleue the paynture/ but the trouthe and the dede/ as men may see by this present Fable/ Of a man & of a lyon which had stryf to gyder & were in grete discencion for to wete and knowe/ whiche of them bothe was more stronger/ ¶The man sayd/ that he was stronger than the lyon/ And for to haue his sayenge veryfyed/ he shewed to the lyon a pyctour/ where as a man had vyctory ouer a lyon/ As the pyctour of Sampson the stronge/ ¶Thenne sayd the lyon to the man/ yf the lyon coude make pyctour good and trewe/ hit had be herin paynted/ how the lyon had had vyctorye of the man/ but now I shalle shewe to the very and trewe wytnesse therof/ The lyon thenne ledde the man to a grete pytte/ And there they fought to gyder/ But the lyon caste the man in to the pytte/ and submytted hym in to his subiection and sayd/ Thow man/ now knowest thow alle the trouthe/ whiche of vs bothe is stronger/ ¶And therfore at the werke is knowen the best and most subtyle werker/

—William Caxton

:35

The Acorn and the Pumpkin

What God does is well done. Without searching
for proof the world over, I find it in pumpkins.

Noticing the size of one, and how delicate
its stem withal, a villager fell to wondering:
"What could the Creator have been thinking of,
putting the pumpkin where he has! Myself,
I would have hung it there, on one of those oaks—
a perfect match: by their fruits ye shall know them!
A pity, Garo, you were not consulted by Him
your curé keeps preaching to you about—
it would have turned out so much the better:
for example, why should the acorn (no larger
than my little fingernail) not be hanging here
in the pumpkin's place? God has made a mistake.
The more I consider how these matters are arranged,
the more obvious it becomes that God was wrong."
Overcome by so much reflection—and so deep—
our man discovers what he needs is sleep:
and straightway under an oak he takes his nap.
An acorn falls—lands on the sleeper's nose.
He wakens, and rubbing his face with one hand
discovers it clinging, still, to his beard.
His throbbing nose compels a change of tune:
"Oh, I'm bleeding! And just suppose," he cries,
"a heavier weight had fallen from the tree—
what if the acorn had been a pumpkin after all?

God willed it otherwise: no doubt He was right,
and now I see the reason." Praising God,
therefore, in all His works, Garo goes home again.

—LA FONTAINE

translated by Richard Howard

Chuang Chou Hunting

Chuang Chou was wandering in the park at Tiao-ling when he saw a peculiar kind of magpie that came flying along from the south. It had a wingspread of seven feet and its eyes were a good inch in diameter. It brushed against Chuang Chou's forehead and then settled down in a grove of chestnut trees. "What kind of bird is that!" exclaimed Chuang Chou. "Its wings are enormous but they get it nowhere; its eyes are huge but it can't even see where it's going!" Then he hitched up his robe, strode forward, cocked his crossbow and prepared to take aim. As he did so, he spied a cicada that had found a lovely spot of shade and had forgotten all about [the possibility of danger to] its body. Behind it, a praying mantis, stretching forth its claws, prepared to snatch the cicada, and it too had forgotten about its own form as it eyed its prize. The peculiar magpie was close behind, ready to make off with the praying mantis, forgetting its own true self as it fixed its eyes on the prospect of gain. Chuang Chou, shuddering at the sight, said, "Ah!—things do nothing but make trouble for each other—one creature calling down disaster on another!" He threw down his crossbow, turned about, and hurried from the park, but the park keeper [taking him for a poacher] raced after him with shouts of accusation.

—CHUANG TZU
translated by Burton Watson

The Mouse's Hole

The god Susanoo shot a humming arrow into a great plain and ordered Ōnamuji to fetch it. As soon as Ōnamuji entered the plain, Susanoo set fire all round the sides. Ōnamuji had no idea how to escape. At this moment a mouse came up to him and said, "The inside is oh so hollow, the outside is oh so narrow." Hearing these words, Ōnamuji stamped on the ground where he stood and opened a hole into which he fell and was hidden until the fire had passed over him. Then the mouse appeared, carrying the humming arrow in his mouth, and presented it to Ōnamuji. The feathers of the arrow had all been chewed up by the mouse's children.

—from the *Kojiki*
translated by IVAN MORRIS

Fables which are peopled by
those who never will perceive
the foolishness of their actions

Marten and the File

A Marten slithering about for food found her way into a bronze foundry and began to lick at a file that lay there. Her tongue was rubbed raw and blood began to fill the grooves. It delighted her so to think she was extracting food from the iron, that she licked more and more vigorously, and lost her tongue altogether.

—AESOP   (*Medieval Prose Polyglot*)
adapted by Karen Kennerly

Nero's Respite

Nero wasn't worried at all when he heard
          what the Delphic Oracle had to say:
"Beware the age of seventy-three."
Plenty of time to enjoy himself.
He's thirty. The respite
the god has given him is quite enough
to cope with future dangers.

Now, a little tired, he'll return to Rome—
but wonderfully tired after that journey
devoted entirely to pleasure:
theaters, garden-parties, stadiums . . .
evenings in the cities of Achaia . . .
above all the delight of naked bodies . . .

So Nero muses. And in Spain Galba
secretly musters and drills his army—
Galba, now in his seventy-third year.

—C. P. CAVAFY

translated by Edmund Keeley and Philip Sherrard

The Two Matches

O ne day there was a traveller in the woods in California, in the dry season, when the Trades were blowing strong. He had ridden a long way, and he was tired and hungry, and dismounted from his horse to smoke a pipe. But when he felt in his pocket, he found but two matches. He struck the first, and it would not light.

"Here is a pretty state of things," said the traveller. "Dying for a smoke; only one match left; and that certain to miss fire! Was there ever a creature so unfortunate? And yet," thought the traveller, "suppose I light this match, and smoke my pipe, and shake out the dottle here in the grass—the grass might catch on fire, for it is dry like tinder; and while I snatch out the flames in front, they might evade and run behind me, and seize upon yon bush of poison oak; before I could reach it, that would have blazed up; over the bush I see a pine tree hung with moss; that too would fly in fire upon the instant to its topmost bough; and the flame of that long torch—how would the trade wind take and brandish that through the inflammable forest! I hear this dell roar in a moment with the joint voice of wind and fire, I see myself gallop for my soul, and the flying conflagration chase and out-flank me through the hills; I see this pleasant forest burn for days, and the cattle roasted, and the springs dried up, and the farmer ruined, and his children cast upon the world. What a world hangs upon this moment!"

With that he struck the match, and it missed fire.

"Thank God," said the traveller, and put his pipe in his pocket.

—ROBERT LOUIS STEVENSON

46:

Drowning Mouse

A mouse fell in a pot of soup which had no lid. Choked by the grease and gasping out his life, he said: "I've done my eating, and my drinking, I've had my fill of all delights; the time has come for me to die."

—BABRIUS

translated by Ben Edwin Perry

The Frog Jealous of the Ox

An Ox, eyed by a lady Frog,
    Stood rarely handsome in her sight.
She, altogether smaller than an egg, agog
With envy, stretched and puffed and struggled that she
      might
    Attain the animal's enormous size,
    Saying: "Look my sister, turn your eyes!
How's this, and what do you say to that? Come, won't this
      do?"
"Not yet." "Now will it?" "Not at all." "Is this a start?"
"No, nothing like it." And the stupid midget blew
    Herself in two, and split apart.

This world is full of people not one whit more sage:
The tradesman's house must vie with noble places,
    The petty prince sends for his embassies,
    The very marquis keeps his page.

—LA FONTAINE
translated by Francis Duke

The Monkey and the Spectacles

A monkey who was graying a little began squinting short-sightedly. He'd heard people say, however, that this particular calamity had dwindled to nothing: One simply wore spectacles. So he selected six or seven kinds. Flipping them over and swinging them around, he tried glasses everywhere. Pressed them to his forehead— no—next strung them along his tail; he sniffed the rims and licked on the glass and *still* the spectacles were useless.

"Absurd," he mutters, "ridiculous. Anyone who pays attention to those quacks is an idiot. Glasses! It's all a lie! Seven are not worth one of my whiskers."

Piqued with frustration, he whacked and whacked the glasses against a rock until only a spray of glittery splinters remained.

—IVAN KRYLOV
translated by Martin Lopez-Morillas and Karen Kennerly

Crow's Fall

When Crow was white he decided the sun was too white.
He decided it glared much too whitely.
He decided to attack it and defeat it.

He got his strength flush and in full glitter.
He clawed and fluffed his rage up.
He aimed his beak direct at the sun's center.

He laughed himself to the center of himself.

And attacked.

At his battle cry trees grew suddenly old,
Shadows flattened.

But the sun brightened—
It brightened, and Crow returned charred black.

He opened his mouth but what came out was charred black.

"Up there," he managed,
"Where white is black and black is white, I won."

—Ted Hughes

The Snail and the Mirror

A snail found a mirror and fell in love with it when he saw how it shone. So he crawled onto its surface and began to lick it. But his caresses only smeared its shining reflections with his slaver and filth. A monkey later saw the mirror scummed in this way and said, "Those who allow themselves to be used by such creatures deserve to be mistreated."

—AESOP   (*early Medieval rescension*)

adapted from Lloyd W. Daley's translation by Karen Kennerly

How the Hair of Women Is Long, the Understanding Short, and What a Ghastly Lack of Appreciation There Is in Them for Genius

A man had a cello with one string over which he drew the bow for hours at a time, holding his finger in one place. His wife endured this noise for seven months, waiting patiently for the man to either die of boredom or destroy the instrument. Inasmuch as neither of these desirable things happened, however, one night she said, in a very quiet voice, too, you may be sure: I have observed that when others play that magnificent instrument, there are four strings over which to draw the bow, and the players move their fingers about continuously. The man stopped playing a moment, looked at his wife wisely, shook his head, and said, You are a woman. Your hair is long, your understanding short. Of course the others move their fingers about constantly. They are looking for the place. I've found it.

—WILLIAM SAROYAN   (*from an old Armenian fable*)

Fable of the Mermaid and the Drunks

All those fellows were there inside
    When she entered, utterly naked.
They had been drinking, and began to spit at her.
Recently come from the river, she understood nothing.
She was a mermaid who had lost her way.
The taunts flowed over her glistening flesh.
Obscenities drenched her golden breasts.
A stranger to tears, she did not weep.
A stranger to clothes, she did not dress.
They poked her with cigarette ends and with burnt corks,
and rolled on the tavern floor in raucous laughter.
She did not speak, since speech was unknown to her.
Her eyes were the color of faraway love,
her arms were matching topazes.
Her lips moved soundlessly in coral light,
and ultimately, she left by that door.
Hardly had she entered the river than she was cleansed,
gleaming once more like a white stone in the rain;
and without a backward look, she swam once more,
swam toward nothingness, swam to her dying.

—PABLO NERUDA
translated by Alastair Reid

Coyote Goes Fishing

Coyote and his wife went fishing and caught a lot of suckers. On their way home, some of the fish were squirming and staring from the bottom of the canoe. Coyote got angry at them. "They are moving their mouths. They're swearing at me!" His wife said that's just the way they are when still half-alive. But Coyote would not believe her. So he threw all the fish back into the river. "I don't want them to swear at me," he whined. And they went home hungry.

—YUROK (*California*)
adapted by Karen Kennerly

The Narrow Spoonful

A fama discovered that virtue was a spherical microbe with a lot of feet. Immediately he gave a large tablespoonful to his mother-in-law. The result was ghastly: the lady ceased and desisted from her sarcastic comments, founded a club for lost Alpine climbers, and in less than two months conducted herself in such an exemplary manner that her daughter's defects, having up till then passed unnoticed, came with great suddenness to the first level of consideration, much to the fama's stupefaction. There was no other recourse than to give a spoonful of virtue to his wife, who abandoned him the same night, finding him coarse, insignificant, and all in all, different from those moral archetypes who floated glittering before her eyes.

The fama thought for a long while and finally swallowed a whole flask of virtue. But all the same, he continued to live alone and sad. When he met his mother-in-law or his wife in the street, they would greet one another respectfully and from afar. They did not even dare to speak to one another. Such was his perfection and their fear of being contaminated.

—JULIO CORTÁZAR
translated by Paul Blackburn

Fables which make social and political statements

Hares and Lions

But if there is one man so superlatively excellent (or several but not enough to make the whole complement of a city) that the goodness and ability of all the rest are simply not to be compared with his (or theirs), such men we take not to be part of the state, but to transcend it . . . The great men might well say what the lions in Antisthene's fable said to the hares who asserted their claim to equality with them—"show us your claws and your teeth" . . .

—ARISTOTLE   *(from The Politics)*
translated by T. A. Sinclair

The hares addressed a public meeting and claimed that all should have equal shares, lions and hares alike. The Lions retorted, "A good speech, Hairy-Feet, but it lacks claws and teeth such as we have."

—AESOP   *(an Augustana rescension)*
adapted from Peter Hanford's translation by Karen Kennerly

The Wasps

Rottenness and decay were fast destroying the noble form of a war horse that had been shot under his bold rider. Ever-active nature made use of the dead form of one of her creatures to give life to others. A swarm of young wasps flew from the tainted carcass. "What godlike descent is ours!" exclaimed the wasps; "we are the off-spring of the magnificent horse, the favorite of Neptune."

Hearing this boasting of the wasps, the writer of the fable was reminded of the modern Italians, who call themselves descendants of the old immortal Romans, because they were born upon their graves.

—G. E. LESSING
translated by James Burns

The Companions of Ulysses

TO MY LORD THE DUKE OF BURGUNDY

Prince, sole object of immortal solicitude,
    Permit my incense as well to perfume your altars.
I bring, somewhat belatedly, these offerings
of my muse: years and labors must be my excuse.
My mind is waning, whereas moment by moment
one perceives how yours waxes ever greater:
not moving, merely, but racing, apparently winged!
The hero who bestows such virtues upon it burns
to show, as well, a prowess in the field of Mars.
He aspires to gain the palm of victory, and glory
would incessantly be his, were it not for one god
who stays his hand, one divinity: our king,
who in a month has become the master of the Rhine;
such speed was at the time a necessity, though
today it would perhaps be regarded as rash.
I say no more: neither Mirth nor Love can be
accused of a preference for speechifying.
And Mirth and Love are everywhere with you,
nor desert your train. Though of course other gods
never fail to keep the upper hand: good sense
and reason everywhere prevail in your domain.
Consult these latter with regard to a matter
concerning the rash and reckless Greeks, who gave
themselves up to charms which turned men into beasts.

The companions of Ulysses, after ten years of strife,
wandered at the wind's will, uncertain of their fate,
landing at last upon an isle where Circe, Apollo's

daughter, reigned and ruled: she offered them
a delicious potation, or so it seemed, though laced
with a terrible poison. The first effect was to
vanquish reason; moments later, their body, their face
assumed the expression and features of animals!
they had turned into bears, lions, elephants,
some grown gigantic, others utterly transformed,
even minuscule: *exemplum, ut talpa.* Only
Ulysses escaped this fate, wise enough to forgo
the malefic brew. And since he united to the wit
the wisdom of a hero, not to mention a sweet tongue,
it came about that the sorceress was stricken
by a poison not unlike her own. Goddesses
say what is on their minds—this one declared
her predilections, and Ulysses was too astute
not to take advantage of such a circumstance.
He convinced Circe to make his Greeks . . . themselves.
"Yet are you so sure that that is what they want?"
the nymph inquired, "go ask them yourself, go on!"
Ulysses obeyed, announcing: "The baleful brew
has an antidote, and I can give it to you,
my friends, provided you wish to become men
once again. Speak, for speech is granted now."
The lion spoke, supposing that he roared:
"I am not such a fool as that—as to renounce
the talents I have just acquired! Claws and fangs
are now mine, by which I tear my enemies
to pieces. I am king of the beasts—why turn
citizen of Ithaca? I would not change my state."
Ulysses went from lion to bear: "Now, brother,
look at you—you who were once so handsome!"
"Yes, look at me, look well," replied the bear

in his own fashion, "I am what a bear should be.
Who says one shape is finer than another?
Is yours so situated as to judge of ours?
Ask the she-bear whether I am handsome now,
and if I displease *you*, take your way and leave
me in peace. I am free, happy, without care,
and in a word, I would not change my state."
Ulysses moved on to the wolf, remarking just in case
he met with a similar response, "My friend,
is it not shameful that a lovely young shepherdess
should bewail the greedy appetite with which you
devour her lambs—you who once fiercely defended
the sheepfolds and led a decent life? Forsake
these forests and become, once more, a human being."
"What for?" the wolf replied. "I see no reason.
You call me carnivore—but am I such, any more
than you? Would you not, were I not here,
have devoured the very creatures the village mourns?
Were I a man, can you say I would have less taste
for slaughter? A word is enough, sometimes, for you
to kill each other off—is not man a wolf to man?
All things considered, I daresay that, crime for crime,
one does better being a wolf than a man. I would not
change my state." Ulysses offered all his cure,
and all responded in the same way, large and small:
freedom, forests, to follow their desires was all
they asked, and more than enough to have.
They believed they were free, following their
passions, though no more than slaves of themselves.

Prince, I should have preferred choosing a subject
in which, for your sake, pleasure and instruction

were combined. Doubtless a splendid plan,
if such a choice had been an easy one.
At length the companions of Ulysses occurred to me—
There are many like them in this world of ours,
Men who must suffer, in deserved punishment,
Alike your disapproval and your disdain.

—LA FONTAINE
translated by Richard Howard

Fish Soup

Ooooh you're such a sweetie, come on, you fattie, just a little, tiny taste."

"Darling, I'm stuffed, really, my stomach hurts . . ."

"Come on, stop it. Another bowl! Is this fish soup? Or is this fish soup?"

"I ate three bowls already."

"Are you an accountant? You like it. I can see, so lick it up. What a chowder! Look at the butter, a real amber, jewels of fat, spots of gold. Look! You're eating poetry. Is this the real thing? Carp, fish pupek, even a piece of sterlet. All right, another spoonful, down the hatch, hurry up! Just one more. Come on, one more. And one more. And one . . . another bowl!"

And so the friendly Damian pressured Foka, his pal; drove him without rest or breathing space. Oh, for some time now this Foka has been oozing like a pig. Nonetheless he lifts another bowl. And . . . with a last gasp . . . swallows everything.

"This is a friend," cries Damian. "Oh God, this is what I call friendship. And you're not up on a high horse either. I know. You're in no hurry to go, come on, so, another bowl!"

And now, poor Foka (who likes his soup but is in anguish, for the stuff just won't go down) grabs belt, hat, and runs, half blind, for home. His foot—from that time hence he doesn't dare to set through Damian's front door.

Writer—your straight forward talent—it's a joy to you.
But—remember friends—consider silence too.
With prose and verse, especially yours, be cautious.
Or else like Damian's soup—ecccch—bblehhh—nauseous.

Fable delivered at our literary circle after one member bored the rest with his tedious long reading.

—IVAN KRYLOV
adapted by Mark Mirsky

A Counsel of Birds for Chusing More Kings

The *Birds* were Mightily Possess'd with an Opinion, that it was utterly Impossible for the *Eagle* alone to Administer Equal Justice to All her Subjects; And upon This Ground, there was a Motion put up, for changing the *Monarchy* into a *Republic*: But an old Cunning *Crow*, that saw further into a Millstone than his Neighbor, with One Word of his Mouth Dash'd the Project. *The more Kings you Have*, says he, *The more Sacks there are to be Fill'd*: And so the Debate fell.

A Fox and a Hedge-Hog

Aesop brought the *Samians* to their Wits again out of a most Desperate Sedition with This Fable.

A *Fox*, upon the Crossing of a River, was forc'd away by the Current into an Eddy, and there he lay with Whole Swarms of Flies, Sucking and Galling of him. There was a *Water Hedge-Hog* (we must Imagine) at hand, that in Pure Pity Offer'd to Beat away the *Flies* from him. No, No, says the *Fox*, Pray let 'em Alone, for the Flies that are upon me now are e'en Bursting-full already, and can do me little more Hurt then they have done: But when

These are gone once, there will be a Company you shall see of Starv'd Hungry Wretches to take their Places, that will not leave so much as One Drop of Blood in the Whole Body of me.

The MORAL: *The Force of a Fable.*

—ROGER L'ESTRANGE

The Ostrich

I am going to fly," exclaimed the gigantic ostrich, while the whole family of birds stood around him in anxious expectation. "I'm going to fly," he said again, widely spreading his insufficient wings, and speeding forward like a ship with expanded sails, without lifting from the ground for a moment.

In this effort, we may trace a poetical likeness of those unpoetical minds, who anticipate extraordinary flight in the opening of their vapid odes, and threaten to ascend above the clouds and stars, yet remain eternally attached to the earth.

—G. E. Lessing
translated by James Burns

Privilege

A certain lion once decided he would issue a decree
    Granting some beasts the right to kill, with full impunity,
And specifying which of them could do it.
    Since it was common practice of the day
    Among those same beasts anyway,
He thought it best to give his sanction to it.
No sooner was the law made public than
The beasts, not even reading it again,
    Got a feast under way:
    Which ever one could kill and flay,
    According to the letter of the law,
    Went out and grabbed at everything he saw.
    How many poor souls perished here
    Was never ascertained, I fear!
Only to the vixen did the thought occur
That from this law one could infer
That those to whom the privilege pertained
Might kill and rob each other, unrestrained!
She found herself in gravest consternation
About her own—and all the beasts'—original elation.
    The vixen said, "The thing
    To do is go
    And ask the king."
    But not directly—no,
The way one asks a king a question: foxily, and weighing
Each word to emphasize what one is saying,
All cunningness and exercising great discretion

In choosing the most polished court expression:
"Do you not find yourself endangered, Royal Highness,
By granting such great power to the beasts in your
     dominion?"
So asked the vixen, but despite her subtlety and slyness,
The lion wouldn't give a yes-or-no opinion.
Then, when according to the lion's calculations,
The new decree for long enough had acted on its own,
The privileged beasts were all sent invitations
Summoning them before the lion's throne.
       And those who were the fattest of them all
       Never returned out of the lion's hall.
The lion told the vixen, "Now, that's what I had in mind
When I granted my strongest beasts a freedom of this
     kind.
Why should I struggle to accumulate
Small bits and pieces of my subjects' fat
When I can let a few beasts put on weight?
The Sultan does exactly that:
He gives his pashas the authorization
To rob and cheat the local population,
       And then he takes his fill
       By handfuls, from the till
Where the supply is more than ample.
I have resolved to follow his example."
The vixen, on the point here of objecting,
And pointing out the evil consequences,
Suddenly came to her senses
By opportunely recollecting
It was the lion she was talking to.
Now I shall give to you
An epigram on tax collectors, who

Can easily be reckoned in among
The pashas' ranks, of which I made brief
     mention. . . .
But like the fox, I just changed my intention,
And think it best to hold my tongue.

—Ivan Khemmitser
translated by Harold Segel

The Frogs Asked for a King

In the days when Athens flourished under a democracy, freedom grown rank disturbed the civic calm, and license relaxed the reins of old-time discipline. Then diverse factions formed a common plot and soon a tyrant rose and seized the citadel, Pisistratus. The Athenians now bewailed their dismal state of servitude, not that their ruler was unkind, but any load is hard to bear for those unused to it. When they began to murmur, Aesop told them this little tale:

"The frogs, while enjoying the freedom of their marshes, called with loud cries on Jupiter to grant them a king, one who should forcibly restrain their lax morality. The father of the gods laughingly bestowed on them a little piece of timber; he hurled it, and when it fell with sudden splash and noisy dashing on the water, the timid tribe was filled with awe. Time passed as it lay there sunk in mud, till one frog chanced to thrust a stealthy head above the pool, and having by reconnaissance learned all about the king, called forth the whole assembly. The frogs, no longer awed, raced through the water to his side. With every insult they defiled it, then sent an embassy to Jove to get another king; for, said they, the one he gave them was no good. Thereupon Jove sent them a water snake, who took to snapping them up one by one with cruel teeth. In vain they tried to flee— they were too sluggish. Fear even took away their power of speech. On the sly, therefore, they made Mercury their messenger to Jove, beseeching him for help in their affliction. Then spoke the Thunderer in reply: 'Since you were unwilling to put up with the good you had, you must put up with this evil.'

"Likewise you, citizens of Athens," said Aesop, "must bear with the evil that you have, lest a greater one befall you."

—PHAEDRUS

translated by Ben Edwin Perry

The Squirrel

A Squirrel served the Lion. What he did, how he managed, one cannot know. Simply: he made the Lion pleased and to please the Lion is no mean task. In return, the Lion promised him a cartload of nuts. He promises—and time lags on. The wretched squirrel goes hungry but, always kept at the Lion's side, he can merely gnash his teeth, and whimper. He looks around. In the forest his friends are flitting back and forth, high above him. The Squirrel takes one cautious step towards a hazelnut tree; he looks . . . Impossible! Now called, now pushed, he's back to serve the Lion.

At length the Squirrel grew old. The Lion was bored with him, and decided to let him go. The Squirrel was pensioned off, and, true to word, got his wagonload of nuts. These nuts were perfect, the finest hoard any squirrel might have. And choice selections, nut for nut. Just one thing was wrong: for years the Squirrel had had no teeth.

—IVAN KRYLOV
translated by Martin Lopez-Morillas and Karen Kennerly

The Rat Recluse

According to a legend of the Levant,
      a rat weary of the world's concerns
took refuge from them in an Edam cheese.
Deep was his solitude, extending equally
in all directions from his central nook.
Herein our new hermit subsisted pretty well,
working foot and fang until he had
food and lodging both: who asks for more?
Big and fat he grew: God blesses those
who dedicate themselves to Him. One day
a pious deputy of the genus Rat
came in search of alms, help was being sought
in foreign lands, against the genus Cat,
for at home Rat City was besieged, and all
inhabitants forced to leave, empty-handed.
Given the need of the beleaguered state,
little enough was asked—surely such aid
would be forthcoming in a day or two?
"My friend," the anchorite replied,
"things of this world mean nothing to me now,
nor can a poor recluse afford much aid—
what more can I do than pray to God
to help you in your dire extremity,
and hope He heeds our prayers all." With which
the new-made saint withdrew and shut his door.

What do you suppose I may have had in mind
by a rat so uncharitable as this?
A monk? Not at all—I meant a dervish:
monks, I assume, are always open-handed.

—LA FONTAINE

translated by Richard Howard

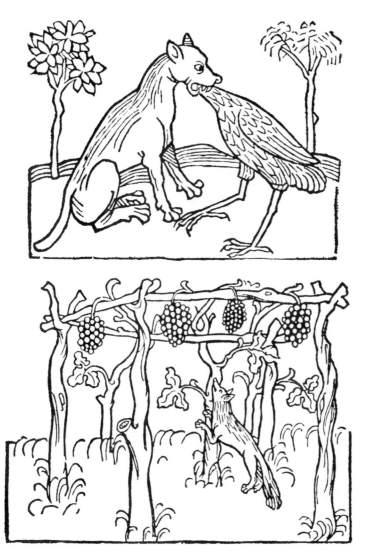

Variant plays on the same fables

Sword-Fish and Whale

Toward the sea turning my troubled eye,
       I saw the fish (if fish I may it clepe)
That makes the sea before his face to flye,
And with his faggie finnes doth seeme to sweepe
       The fomie waues out of the dreadfull deep,
The huge *Leviathan*, dame Natures wonder,
Making his sport, that manie makes to weep:
A sword-fish small him from the rest did sunder,
       That in his throat him pricking softly vnder,
His wide Abysse him forced forth to spewe,
That all the sea did roare like heauens thunder,
And all the waues were stain'd with filthie hewe.
       Hereby I learned haue, not to despise,
       What euer thing seemes small in common eyes.

Elephant and the Ant

Soone after this I saw an Elephant,
       Adorn'd with bells and bosses gorgeouslie,
That on his backe did beare (as batteilant)
A gilden towre, which shone exceedinglie;
       That he himselfe through foolish vanitie,
Both for his rich attire, and goodly forme,

:81

Was puffed vp with passing surquedrie,
And shortly gan all other beasts to scorne,
    Till that a little Ant, a silly worme,
Into his nosthrils creeping, so him pained,
That casting downe his towres, he did deforme
Both borrowed pride, and natiue beautie stained.
    Let therefore nought that great is, therein glorie,
    Sith so small thing his happiness may varie.

—EDMUND SPENSER

Story of the Old Wolf
in seven fables

[1]

The bad wolf had grown old, and decided that it was expedient to live on good terms with the shepherds. So he made his way to the shepherd whose flocks were closest to the wolf's lair.

"Shepherd," he said, "you call me the bloodthirsty robber I really am not. To be sure, I have to depend on your sheep when I am hungry, because hunger hurts. But just preserve me from hunger; keep me well fed, and you'll have reason to change your mind about me. For I really am the tamest and gentlest of animals when I've eaten my fill."

"When you've eaten your fill? That may well be so," the shepherd replied; "but when have you ever eaten your fill? You and avarice never do. So make yourself scarce!"

[2]

The rejected wolf came to another shepherd.

"You know, shepherd," was his opening gambit, "that I could kill off many of your sheep in the course of a year. If you'll simply give me six sheep a year I shall be content. You can then sleep in peace and get rid of your dogs."

"Six sheep?" said the shepherd. "Why, that's a whole flock!"

"Well, as a special concession to you, I'll make it five," said the wolf.

"You're joking. Five sheep! That's almost more than I sacrificed to Pan in a full year."

"Not even four, then?" the wolf went on; and the shepherd contemptuously shook his head.

"Three?—Two?—"

"Not a single one," was the final answer. "For it would be the height of folly for me to pay tribute money to an enemy from whom I can protect myself by being wary."

[3]

"Third time lucky," thought the wolf, and came to a third shepherd.

"I am deeply distressed," he said, "that you shepherds decry me as the most cruel and unscrupulous of animals. Now I'm going to prove to you, Montanus, what an injustice you do me. Give me one sheep a year, and your flock shall graze unharmed in that wood which no one but myself makes unsafe. That's what I said: one sheep. A mere trifle. Could I be more generous, more distinterested than that? You're laughing, shepherd? What are you laughing about?"

"Oh, nothing—nothing at all. How old are you, dear friend?" the shepherd asked.

"What's my age got to do with you? Still the right age, anyway, to kill off your favorite lambs."

"Keep calm, old wolf! I'm sorry that you've made your proposal just a few years too late. Your missing teeth give you away. You're pretending to be disinterested only so that you can gorge yourself more comfortably, and with less danger."

[4]

The wolf grew angry, but composed himself and went on to the fourth shepherd. That one had just lost his faithful sheepdog, and the wolf took advantage of this circumstance.

"Shepherd," he said, "I have fallen out with my brothers in the wood, and so badly that we shall never be reconciled in all eternity. You know how much you have to fear from them. But if you'll take me into your service in place of your dead dog, I can guarantee that they won't so much as look awry at a single sheep of yours."

"So you're offering to protect my sheep from your brothers in the wood?"

"What else could I mean? Of course."

"That wouldn't be a bad thing. Only, if I were to take you on for my flock, who would then protect my poor sheep from you? Tell me that. To welcome a thief into one's house, so as to be safe from the thieves outside, that's what we men would call—"

"I get the point," said the wolf; "you're starting to moralize. Goodbye."

[5]

"If only I weren't so old," the wolf muttered to himself. "But unfortunately there's nothing I can do about time." And so he came to the fifth shepherd.

"Do you know me, shepherd?" asked the wolf.

"I know your sort, in any case," the shepherd replied.

"My sort? I very much doubt that. I am so extraordinary a wolf that I'm worthy of your friendship, and that of all shepherds."

"How extraordinary are you, then?"

"I could never kill or eat a living sheep, even if it cost me my life. I feed only on dead sheep. Isn't that virtuous of me? So always allow me to come to your flock from time to time and ask you whether—"

"Don't waste more words," said the shepherd. "You'd have to eat no sheep at all, not even dead ones, for me not to be your enemy. An animal that begins by eating my dead sheep will soon be taught by hunger to regard sick sheep as dead ones, and healthy ones as sick. Don't count on my friendship, therefore, and be off!"

[6]

"I can see that I shall have to stake my dearest possession to attain my ends," the wolf thought, and came to the sixth shepherd.

"Shepherd," he asked, "how do you like my fur?"

"Your fur? Let me see. Yes, it's fine; our dogs can't have got their teeth into you very often."

"Well, listen, shepherd; I am old, and probably shan't be going on very much longer. Feed me to death; and I'll leave you my fur."

"So that's it," said the shepherd. "So you too have got wise to old misers' tricks, have you? But no; in the end your fur would cost me seven times more than it's worth. If you're serious about wanting to make me a present, just hand it over, straight away." Saying this, the shepherd seized his club, and the wolf fled.

[7]

"Hard-hearted, merciless lot!" howled the wolf, growing enraged. "I will die as their enemy, then, before hunger kills me; for that's how they want it."

He ran off, broke into the shepherds' homes, pulled their children to the ground, and it was not without a hard struggle that the shepherds clubbed him to death.

Then the wisest of them said: "It was wrong of us, I think, to reduce the old robber to this extremity and to deprive him of all possible means to reform, however belated and enforced."

—G. E. LESSING
translated by Michael Hamburger

The Fox and the Crow

A crow, perched in a tree with a piece of cheese in his beak, attracted the eye and nose of a fox. "If you can sing as prettily as you sit," said the fox, "then you are the prettiest singer within my scent and sight." The fox had read somewhere, and somewhere, and somewhere else, that praising the voice of a crow with a cheese in his beak would make him drop the cheese and sing. But this is not what happened to this particular crow in this particular case.

"They say you are sly and they say you are crazy," said the crow, having carefully removed the cheese from his beak with the claws of one foot, "but you must be nearsighted as well. Warblers wear gay hats and colored jackets and bright vests, and they are a dollar a hundred. I wear black and I am unique." He began nibbling the cheese, dropping not a single crumb.

"I am sure you are," said the fox, who was neither crazy nor nearsighted, but sly. "I recognize you, now that I look more closely, as the most famed and talented of all birds, and I fain would hear you tell about yourself, but I am hungry and must go."

"Tarry awhile," said the crow quickly, "and share my lunch with me." Whereupon he tossed the cunning fox the lion's share of the cheese, and began to tell about himself. "A ship that sails without a crow's nest sails to doom," he said. "Bars may come and bars may go, but crow bars last forever. I am the pioneer of flight, I am the map maker. Last, but never least, my flight is known to scientists and engineers, geometrists and scholars, as the shortest distance between two points. Any two points," he concluded arrogantly.

"Oh, every two points, I am sure," said the fox. "And thank you for the lion's share of what I know you could not spare." And with this he trotted away into the woods, his appetite appeased, leaving the hungry crow perched forlornly in the tree.

The MORAL: *'Twas true in Aesop's time, and La Fontaine's, and now, no one else can praise thee quite so well as thou.*

VARIATIONS ON THE THEME

I

A fox, attracted by the scent of something, followed his nose to a tree in which sat a crow with a piece of cheese in his beak. "Oh, cheese," said the fox scornfully. "That's for mice."

The crow removed the cheese with his talons and said, "You always hate the thing you cannot have, as, for instance, grapes."

"Grapes are for the birds," said the fox haughtily. "I am an epicure, a gourmet, and a gastronome."

The embarrassed crow, ashamed to be seen eating mouse food by a great specialist in the art of dining, hastily dropped the cheese. The fox caught it deftly, swallowed it with relish, said *"Merci,"* politely, and trotted away.

II

A fox had used all his blandishments in vain, for he could not flatter the crow in the tree and make him drop the cheese he held in his beak. Suddenly, the crow tossed the cheese to the astonished fox. Just then the farmer, from whose kitchen the loot had been stolen, appeared, carrying a rifle, looking for the robber. The fox turned and ran for the woods. "There goes the guilty son of a vixen now!" cried the crow, who, in case you do not happen to know it, can see the glint of sunlight on a gun barrel at a greater distance than anybody.

III

This time the fox, who was determined not to be outfoxed by a crow, stood his ground and did not run when the farmer appeared, carrying a rifle and looking for the robber.

"The teeth marks in this cheese are mine," said the fox, "but the beak marks were made by the true culprit up there in the tree. I submit this cheese in evidence, as Exhibit A, and bid you and the criminal a very good day." Whereupon he lit a cigarette and strolled away.

IV

In the great and ancient tradition, the crow in the tree with the cheese in his beak began singing, and the cheese fell into the fox's lap. "You sing like a shovel," said the fox, with a grin, but the crow pretended not to hear and cried out, "Quick, give me back the cheese! Here comes the farmer with his rifle!"

"Why should I give you back the cheese?" the wily fox demanded.

"Because the farmer has a gun, and I can fly faster than you can run."

So the frightened fox tossed the cheese back to the crow, who ate it, and said, "Dearie me, my eyes are playing tricks on me—or am I playing tricks on you? Which do you think?" But there was no reply, for the fox had slunk away into the woods.

—James Thurber

Dog and His Shadow

A dog stole a piece of meat from a kitchen and with it ran beside the river. Seeing in the stream the shadow, much larger than the meat itself, he let go the meat and dashed for the shadow. This he did not find, nor the meat that he had dropped. Still hungry he crossed back the way he came.

—BABRIUS

translated by Ben Edwin Perry

Chüang Shu-liang in the Moonlight

There was a man named Chüang Shu-liang who lived south of Hsia-Shou. One night he was walking in the moonlight, when, glancing down and seeing his shadow, he took it for a crouching ghost. Looking up, he caught sight of his own hair and took it for a devil standing over him. He whirled around and started running, and when he reached his home he fell unconscious and died.

—Hsün Tzu
translated by Burton Watson

A Country Mouse and a Town Mouse

country mouse once gave a town mouse a welcome
        In his poor hole, or so it says in the story;
An old host, and the other an old friend.
But able to open that straitened heart of his
In hospitality. Not to lengthen my tale,
He did not grudge him the chick-peas stowed away
Or the long oats, but bringing along in his mouth
A dried raisin and half-eaten scraps of bacon
Gave them to him, hoping with varied fare
To overcome the daintiness shown by his guest,
Who would barely touch with his fastidious tooth
Each morsel before him; the householder, sprawled in the
        meantime
On fresh straw, had a meal of darnel and spelt,
Leaving the choicer bits of the feast for his friend.
At length the town mouse spoke to him. "Friend," said he,
"How can you like this laborious life of yours
On the ridge of a steep coppice? To put behind you
The wild woods for the town, for the world of men—
Is that what you want? Then follow the road with me,
You take my word! Since all the creatures on earth
Now living have souls allotted them doomed to die,
And none can escape from death, whether little or great,
That's all the more reason for you to live happy, good sir,
In pleasant surroundings, as long as you're able to do so;
Spend your life in the thought of how brief your time is!"
These words impressed the country bumpkin, and nimbly

He leaped from his home; the pair of them then, as
    planned,
Pursued their journey, eager to creep by night
Under the city walls. And now the night
Was occupying the middle space of the sky,
When both set foot in a wealthy house, where covers
Dyed bright scarlet gleamed upon ivory couches.
There had been a magnificent banquet the evening
    before,
And a good many courses, left over, were piled up in
    baskets
That stood near by. So when the town mouse had placed
His guest from the country stretched out on a purple
    cover,
He darted about like a host well-girded for action
And served course after course, fulfilling the duties
That fall to a home-bred slave, and tasting beforehand
Whatever he brought to the table. The one on the couch,
Overjoyed at the change in his fortune, was happily
    playing
His part as guest in the midst of the good things,
When all of a sudden a terrible banging of doors
Shook them both from their couches. Stricken with fear,
They scampered all over the room, half dead with fright,
And palpitating the more as the lofty hall
Rang with the baying of huge Molossian hounds.
Then said he from the country: "I have no use
For a life like this. Goodbye. My hole in the wood,
Safe from surprise, shall console me with homely vetch."

—HORACE
translated by Michael Oakley

Feld Mowse and Towny Mowse

My mothers maydes when they did sowe and
    spynne,
    They sang sometyme a song of the feld mowse,
    That forbicause her lyvelood was but thynne,
Would nedes goo seke her townysshe systers howse.
    She thought her self endured to much pain,
    The stormy blastes her cave so sore did sowse,
That when the forowse swymmed with the rain
    She must lye cold and whete in sorry plight;
    And wours then that, bare meet there did remain
To comfort her when she her howse had dight,
    Sometyme a barly corne, sometyme a bene,
    For which she laboured hard boeth daye and nyght,
In harvest tyme whilest she myght goo and glyne;
    And when her stoore was stroyed with the flodd,
    Then wellawaye! for she vndone was clene.
Then was she fayne to take in stede of fode
    Slepe if she myght her hounger to begile.
    'My syster' (quoth she) 'hath a lyving good,
And hens from me she dwelleth not a myle.
    In cold and storme she lieth warme and dry
    In bed of downe; the dyrt doeth not defile
Her tender fote. She laboureth not as I.
    Richely she fedeth and at the richemans cost,
    And for her meet she nydes not crave nor cry.
By se, by land, of delicates the moost
    Her Cater sekes and spareth for no perell;
    She fedeth on boyled, bacon meet, and roost,

And hath therof neither charge nor travaill;
    And when she list the licor of the grape
    Doeth glad her hert, till that her belly swell.'
And at this jorney she maketh but a jape;
    So fourth she goeth trusting of all this welth
    With her syster her part so for to shape
That if she myght kepe her self in helth
    To lyve a Lady while her liff doeth last.
    And to the dore now is she come by stelth,
And with her foote anon she scrapeth full fast.
    Th'othre for fere durst not well scarse appere,
    Of every noyse so was the wretche agast.
At last she asked softly who was there,
    And in her langage as well as she cowd,
    'Pepe,' quoth the othre syster, 'I ame here.'
'Peace,' quoth the towny mowse, 'Why spekest thou so
        lowde?'
    And by the hand she toke her fayer and well.
    'Welcome,' quoth she, 'my sister by the Roode!'
She fested her, that joy it was to tell
    The faere they had: they drancke the wyne so clere.
    And as to pourpose now and then it fell
She chered her with 'How, syster, what chiere?'
    Amyddes this joye befell a sorry chaunce
    That well awaye! the straunger bought full dere
The fare she had; for as she loked ascaunce,
    Vnder a stole she spied two stemyng Ise
    In a rownde hed with sherp erys. In Fraunce
Was never mowse so ferd for tho the vnwise
    Had not Isene suche a beest before,
    Yet had nature taught her after her gyse
To knowe her ffoo and dred him evermore.

The towney mowse fled: she knewe whether to goo.
Th'othre had no shift but wonders sore,
Fferd of her liff: at home she wyshed her tho,
And to the dore, alas, as she did skippe—
Thevyn it would, lo, and eke her chaunce was so—
At the threshold her sely fote did trippe,
And ere she myght recover it again
The traytor Catt had caught her by the hippe
And made her there against her will remain,
That had forgotten her poure suretie and rest
For semyng welth wherin she thought to rayne.
Alas, my Poynz, how men do seke the best,
And fynde the wourst by error as they stray!

—THOMAS WYATT

The Hedgehog and the Hare

One day the hare met the hedgehog and he said: "You wouldn't be so bad, hedgehog, except that your legs are crooked, and you stumble."

The hedgehog grew angry and said: "What are you laughing at? My crooked legs can run faster than your straight ones. Just let me go home for a moment, and then you and I shall run a race!"

The hedgehog went home and said to his wife: "I had an argument with the hare and we're going to run a race."

The hedgehog's wife said: "You must be out of your mind! How can you run a race with the hare? His legs are nimble, while yours are crooked and slow!"

"His legs may be nimble," replied the hedgehog, "but my wits are nimble. You have only to do as I tell you. Now, let us go to the field."

They went to the plowed field where the hare was waiting.

"You hide at this end of the furrow," said the hedge-hog to his wife. "The hare and I will start from the other end. As soon as he begins to run I'll turn around and go back. When he reaches this end you come out and say: 'I've been waiting here a long time for you!' He can't tell one of us from the other, and he'll think you are me."

The hedgehog's wife hid in the furrow, and the hare and the hedgehog started their race from the other end.

As soon as the hare began to run, the hedgehog turned back and hid in the furrow. When the hare reached the other end, what did he see?—There sat the hedgehog's wife!

"I've been waiting for you a long time!" she said.

"What a miracle!" thought the hare, who could not tell her from her husband. "How could he have outrun me?"

"Come," he said aloud, "let's run again!"

"All right!"

The hare set off, and when he arrived at the other end, what did he see?—There sat the hedgehog!

"Well, brother," he said, "at last you're here! I've been waiting a long time!"

"What a miracle!" thought the hare. "No matter how fast I run, he always outruns me!"

"Come," he said, "let us run again, and this time you won't beat me!"

"All right!" said the hedgehog.

The hare hopped away as fast as he could, but again the hedgehog sat waiting at the end of the furrow.

And thus the hare continued hopping from one end of the furrow to the other until he was exhausted.

He finally gave up and said that henceforth he would never argue again.

—LEO TOLSTOY

Heron and Humming-Bird

Heron and Humming-Bird lived on the shores of the ocean in the east. One day Humming-Bird came to Heron, and said, "Let us race." Heron answered, "I can't fly. I can't do anything." But Humming-Bird kept teasing him to race and finally Heron gave in. They agreed to race from the ocean in the east to the ocean in the west; so they placed themselves at the edge of the water, and began. Heron had barely lifted his wings when Humming-Bird was out of sight, and he raised himself slowly, flapping along at an even pace. When darkness came, Humming-Bird went to a tree and stopped there for the night; but Heron kept steadily on, and shortly before daylight he was at the place where Humming-Bird was sitting. Day came—Heron had traveled a long distance ahead and the sun was well up before Humming-Bird passed him. Next night, Humming-Bird had to rest again, and again Heron went by him, but this time about midnight. Humming-Bird did not pass him again until noon. The third night, Heron caught up with Humming-Bird before midnight, and Humming-Bird did not go by him until late evening. But then he had to stop once more and Heron soon overtook him. So Heron got to the western ocean far ahead. It was early in the morning when he arrived, and he began hunting for fish. Humming-Bird did not come until noon. Then Humming-Bird said to Heron, "I did not believe you could get here first; for I can dart all around you and all over you."

—MUSKOGEE   (*Southeastern United States*)

The Crocodile
in Need of a Surgeon

The crocodile, which lives in the River Nilus, hath a worm breeds i' th' teeth of 't, which puts it to extreme anguish: a little bird, no bigger than a wren, is barber-surgeon to this crocodile; flies into the jaws of 't, picks out the worm, and brings present remedy. The fish, glad of ease, but ungrateful to her that did it, that the bird may not talk largely of her abroad for non-payment, closeth her chaps, intended to swallow her, and so put her to perpetual silence. But nature, loathing such ingratitude, hath armed this bird with a quill or prick on the head, top o' th' which wounds the crocodile i' th' mouth, forceth her open her bloody prison, and away flies the pretty tooth-picker from her cruel patient.

—JOHN WEBSTER

Patient Forbearance

A wolf once got a bone stuck in his throat.
He gave a heron a promissory note
of recompense if with his neck a-stretch
he pulled the bone out and relieved the wretch.
After the extraction, heron claimed his fee.
Wolf smiled a biting smile. "Enough," said he,
"you are already paid for your first-aid,
from a wolf's gullet getting your noodle free."

—BABRIUS

translated by Robert Fitzgerald

The Dog and the Dates

When a dog crept into an orchard intent on stealing dates, the owner spotted him, and chased him out on to the road. He and his men continued to fill their sacks with the harvest. That evening, as they walked home shouldering the abundant fruit, the owner stopped for a moment and said to the dog: "Really, the dates are quite bitter." "I am not such a fool!" whined the dog by the roadside, "It is one thing to chase me away, quite another to insult me!"

—SUMER

closely adapted by Karen Kennerly from a
partially indecipherable text

The Fox and the Grapes

There was a time, when a *Fox* would have ventur'd as far for a Bunch of Grapes as for a shoulder of *Mutton*, and it was a *Fox* of those days, and of that palate, that stood gaping under the vine, and licking his lips at a most delicious cluster of *Grapes* that he had spy'd out there; he fetched a Hundred and a Hundred leaps at it, 'till at last, when he was as weary as a Dog, and found that there was no good to be done; Hang 'em (says he) they are as Sour as *Crabs*; and so away he went, turning off the disappointment with a Jest.

—Roger L'Estrange

Fox and Grapes

A Gascon—or some say a Norman—Fox, near dead
    Of hunger, came upon a grapevine in the sun
That on a trellis overhead
Bore grapes of warm vermillion.
The good man might have found a banquet very pleasant,
    But he couldn't stretch that high,
And so he said: "Those grapes are sour, fit food for a
    peasant."

Better than to howl, say I.

—LA FONTAINE
translated by Francis Duke

The Fox and the Grapes

I know a poet to whom the screaming admiration of his petty imitators does far more harm than the envious contempt of his critics.

"But they're sour!" said the fox about a bunch of grapes which he had long been trying in vain to reach. A sparrow heard this and said, "You say they're sour, those grapes? They don't look sour to me!" He flew over and tasted them and found them uncommonly sweet, whereupon he called hundreds of his greedy brothers. "Come and taste them!" he cried, "come and taste them! The fox calls these wonderful grapes sour!"

All the sparrows tasted them, and in a short while the grapes were so picked at and mauled about that no fox ever jumped up at them again.

—G. E. LESSING
translated by James Burns

The Fox and the Grapes

One day a ferocious bunch of grapes were hanging idly on a grape vine. These weren't any ordinary grapes because each grape had a different personality. All of their personalities resulted in a demolition squad of grapes.

A very unconcerned fox came walking by without a care in the world. Suddenly he was frightened by the grapes, which were making an attempt to eat the fox. The grapes tugged at the vine so as to stretch far enough to reach him. But each time the fox would move an inch away. The grapes were grunting and large beads of sweat rolled off them in a river-like fashion. The grapes were at the end of their vine; they could stretch no further. Then at that moment the fox appeared even more delicious than before. Unable to control their desire for fresh meat, the grapes stretched with all their might until the vine broke. The grapes lay on the ground and were later eaten by the fox.

The MORAL: *It doesn't pay to stretch your neck out, or Don't stretch until you come to the end of your vine.*

—DONALD GEAR, *a New York high school student*

The Mookse and the Gripes

Gentes and laitymen, fullstoppers and semicolonials, hybreds and lubberds!

Eins within a space and a wearywide space it wast ere wohned a Mookse. The onesomeness wast alltolonely, archunsitslike, broady oval, and a Mookse he would a walking go (My hood! cries Antony Romeo), so one grandsumer evening, after a great morning and his good supper of gammon and spittish, having flabelled his eyes, pilleoled his nostrils, vacticanated his ears and palliumed his throats, he put on his impermeable, seized his impugnable, harped on his crown and stepped out of his immobile *De Rure Albo* (socolled becauld it was chalkfull of masterplasters and had borgeously letout gardens strown with cascadas, pintacostecas, horthoducts and currycombs) and set off from Ludstown *a spasso* to see how badness was badness in the weirdest of all pensible ways.

As he set off with his father's sword, his *lancia spezzata*, he was girded on, and with that between his legs and his tarkeels, our once in only Bragspear, he clanked, to my clinking, from veetoes to threetop, every inch of an immortal.

He had not walked over a pentiadpair of parsecs from his azylum when at the turning of the Shinshone Lanteran near Saint Bowery's-without-his-Walls he came (secunding to the one one oneth of the propecies, *Amnis Limina Permanent*) upon the most unconsciously boggy-looking stream he ever locked his eyes with. Out of the colliens it took a rise by daubing itself Ninon. It looked little and it smelt of brown and it thought in narrows and it talked showshallow. And as it rinn it dribbled like any lively purliteasy: *My, my, my! Me and me! Little down dream don't I love thee!*

And, I declare, what was there on the yonder bank of the stream that would be a river, parched on a limb of the olum, bolt downright, but the Gripes? And no doubt he was fit to be dried for why had he not been having the juice of his times?

His pips had been neatly all drowned on him; his polps were charging odours every older minute; he was quickly for getting the dresser's desdaign on the flyleaf of his frons; and he was quietly for giving the bailiff's distrain on to the bulkside of his *cul de Pompe*. In all his specious heavings, as be lived by Optimus Maximus, the Mookse had never seen his Dubville brooder-on-low so nigh to a pickle.

Adrian (that was the Mookse now's assumptinome) stuccstill phiz-à-phiz to the Gripes in an accessit of aurignacian. But All-mookse must to Moodend much as All-routs, austereways or wastersways, in roaming run through Room. Hic sor a stone, singularly illud, and on hoc stone Seter satt huc sate which it filled quite poposterously and by acclammitation to its fullest justotoryum and whereopum with his unfallable encyclicling upom his alloilable, diupetriark of the wouest, and the athemyst-sprinkled pederect he always walked with, *Deusdedit*, cheek by jowel with his frisherman's blague, *Bellua Triumphanes*, his everyway addedto wallat's collectium, for yea longer he lieved yea broader he betaught of it, the fetter, the summe and the haul it cost, he looked the first and last micahlike laicness of Quartus the Fifth and

Quintus the Sixth and Sixtus the Seventh giving allnight sitting to Lio the Faultyfindth.

—Good appetite us, sir Mookse! How do you do it? cheeped the Gripes in a wherry whiggy maudelenian woice and the jackasses all within bawl laughed and brayed for his intentions for they knew their sly toad lowry now. I am rarumominum blessed to see you, my dear mouster. Will you not perhopes tell me everything if you are pleased, sanity? All about aulne and lithial and allsall allinall about awn and liseias? Ney?

Think of it! O miserendissimest retempter! A Gripes!

—Rats! bullowed the Mookse most telesphorously, the concionator, and the sissymusses and the zozzymusses in their robenhauses quailed to hear his tardeynois at all for you cannot wake a silken nouse out of a hoarse oar. Blast yourself and your anathomy infairioriboos! No, hang you for an animal rurale! I am superbly in my supremest poncif! Abase you, baldyqueens! Gather behind me, satraps! Rots!

—I am till infinity obliged with you, bowed the Gripes, his whine having gone to his palpruy head. I am still always having a wish on all my extremities. By the watch, what is the time, pace?

Figure it! The pining peever! To a Mookse!

—Ask my index, mund my achilles, swell my obolum, woshup my nase serene, answered the Mookse, rapidly by turning clement, urban, eugenious and celestian in the formose of good grogory humours. Quote awhore? That is quite about what I came on *my* missions with *my* intentions *laudibiliter* to settle with *you*, barbarousse. Let thor be orlog. Let Pauline be Irene. Let you be

Beeton. And let me be Los Angeles. Now measure your length. Now estimate my capacity. Well, sour? Is this space of our couple of hours too dimensional for you, temporiser? Will you give you up? *Como? Fuert it?*

Sancta Patientia! You should have heard the voice that answered him! *Culla vosellina.*

—I was just thinkling upon that, swees Mooksey, but, for all the rime on my raisins, if I connow make my submission, I cannos give you up, the Gripes whimpered from nethermost of his wanhope. Ishallassoboundbewilsothoutoosezit. My tumble, loudy bullocker, is my own. My velicity is too fit in one stockend. And my spetial inexshellsis the belowing things ab ove. But I will never be abler to tell Your Honoriousness (here he near lost his limb) though my corked father was bott a pseudowaiter, whose o'cloak you ware.

Incredible! Well, hear the inevitable.

—*Your* temple, *sus in cribro!* Semperexcommunicambiambisumers. Turgurios-in-Newrobe or Tukurias-in-Ashies. Novarome, my creature, blievend bleives. My building space in lyonine city is always to let to leonlike Men, the Mookse in a most consistorous allocution pompifically with immediate jurisdiction constantinently concludded (what a crammer for the shapewrucked Gripes!). And I regret to proclaim that it is out of my temporal to help you from being killed by inchies, (what a thrust!), as we first met each other newwhere so airly. (Poor little sowsieved subsquashed Gripes! I begin to feel contemption for him!). My side, thank decretals, is as safe as motherour's houses, he continued, and I can seen from my holeydome what it is to be wholly sane. Unionjok and be joined to yok! Parysis, *tu sais*, crucycrooks, belongs to him who parises himself. And there I must leave you subject for the pressing. I can prove that against you, weight a momentum, mein goot enemy! or Cospol's not our star. I bet you this dozen odd. This foluminous dozen odd. *Quas primas*—but 'tis bitter to compote my knowledge's fructos of. Tomes.

Elevating, to give peint to his blick, his jewelled pederect to the allmysty cielung, he luckystruck blueild out of a few shouldbe santillants, a cloister of starabouts over Maples, a lucciolys in Teresa street and a stopsign before Sophy Barratt's, he gaddered togodder the odds docence of his vellumes, gresk, letton and russicruxian, onto the lapse of his prolegs, into umfullth one-scuppered, and sat about his widerproof. He proved it well who-onearth dry and drysick times, and *vremiament, tu cesses,* to the extinction of Niklaus altogether (Niklaus Alopysius having been the once Gripes's popwilled nimbum) by Neuclidius and Inexagoras and Mumfsen and Thumpsem, by Orasmus and by Amenius, by Anacletus the Jew and by Malachy the Augurer and by the Cappon's collection and after that, with Cheekee's gelatine and Alldaybrandy's formolon, he reproved it ehrltogether when not in that order sundering in some different order, alter three thirty and a hundred times by the binomial dioram and the penic walls and the ind, the Inklespill legends and the rure, the rule of the hoop and the blessons of expedience and the jus, the jugicants of Pontius Pilax and all the mummyscrips in Sick Bokes' Juncroom and the Chapters for the Cunning of the Chapters of the Conning Fox by Tail.

While that Mooksius with preprocession and with proprecession, duplicitly and diplussedly, was promulgating ipsofacts and sadcontras this raskolly Gripos he had allbust seceded in monophysicking his illsobordunates. But asawfulas he had caught his base semenoyous sarchnaktiers to combuccinate upon the silipses of his aspillouts and the acheporeoozers of his haggyown pneumax to synerethetise with the breadchestviousness of his sweeatovular ducose sofarfully the loggerthuds of his sakellaries were fond at variance with the synodals of his somepooliom and his babskissed nepogreasymost got the hoof from his philioquus.

—Efter thousand yaws, O Gripes con my sheepskins, yow will be belined to the world, enscayed Mookse the pius.

—Ofter thousand yores, amsered Gripes the gregary, be the goat of MacHammud's, yours may be still, O Mookse, more botheared.

—Us shall be chosen as the first of the last by the electress of Vale Hollow, obselved the Mookse nobily, for par the unicum of Elelijiacks, Us am in Our stabulary and that is what Ruby and Roby fall for, blissim.

The Pills, the Nasal Wash (Yardly's), the Army Man Cut, as british as bondstrict and as straightcut as when that brokenarched traveller from Nuzuland . . .

—Wee, cumfused the Gripes limply, shall not even be the last of the first, wee hope, when oust are visitated by the Veiled Horror. And, he added: Mee are relying entirely, see the fortethurd of Elissabed, on the weightiness of mear's breath. Puffut!

Unsightbared embouscher, relentless foe to social and business succes! (Hourihaleine) It might have been a happy evening but . . .

And they viterberated each other, *cants et coluber*

with the wildest ever wielded since Tarriestinus lashed
Pissasphaltium.

—Unuchorn!

—Ungulant!

—Uvuloid!

—Uskybeak!

And bullfolly answered volleyball.

Nuvoletta in her lightdress, spunn of sixteen shim-
mers, was looking down on them, leaning over the bannistars and listening all she childishly could. How she
was brightened when Shouldrups in his glaubering hoch-
skied his welkinstuck and how she was overclused when
Kneesknobs on his zwivvel was makeacting such a paulse
of himshelp! She was alone. All her nubied companions
were asleeping with the squirrels. Their mivver, Mrs
Moonan, was off in the Fuerst quarter scrubbing the
backsteps of Number 28. Fuvver, that Skand, he was up
in Norwood's sokaparlour, eating oceans of Voking's
Blemish. Nuvoletta listened as she reflected herself,
though the heavenly one with his constellatria and his
emanations stood between, and she tried all she tried to
make the Mookse look up at her (but *he* was fore too
adiaptotously farseeing) and to make the Gripes hear how
coy she could be (though he was much too schystimatically
auricular about *his ens* to heed her) but it was all mild's
vapour moist. Not even her feignt reflection, Nuvoluccia,
could they toke their gnoses off for their minds with in-
trepifide fate and bungless curiasty, were conclaved with
Heliogobbleus and Commodus and Enobarbarus and
whatever the coordinal dickens they did as their damp-
rauch of papyrs and buchstubs said. As if that was their
spiration! As if theirs could duiparate her queendim! As

if she would be third perty to search on search proceedings! She tried all the winsome wonsome ways her four winds had taught her. She tossed her sfumastelliacinous hair like *la princesse de la Petite Bretagne* and she rounded her mignons arms like Mrs Cornwallis-West and she smiled over herself like the beauty of the image of the pose of the daughter of the queen of the Emperour of Irelande and she sighed after herself as were she born to bride with Tristis Tristior Tristissimus. But, sweet madonine, she might fair as well have carried her daisy's worth to Florida. For the Mookse, a dogmad Accanite, were not apposed and the Gripes, a dubliboused Catalick, wis pinefully obliviscent.

—I see, she sighed. There are menner.

The siss of the whisp of the sigh of the softzing at the stir of the ver grose O arundo of a long one in midias reeds: and shades began to glidder along the banks, greepsing, greepsing, duusk unto duusk, and it was as glooming as gloaming could be in the waste of all peacable worlds. Metamnisia was allsoonome coloroform brune; citherior spiane an eaulande, innemorous and unnumerose. The Mookse had a sound eyes right but he could not all hear. The Gripes had light ears left yet he could but ill see. He ceased. And he ceased, tung and trit, and it was neversoever so dusk of both of them. But still Moo thought on the deeps of the undths he would profoundth come the morrokse and still Gri feeled of the scripes he would escipe if by grice he had luck enoupes.

Oh, how it was duusk! From Vallee Maraia to Grasya-plaina, dormimust echo! Ah dew! Ah dew! It was so duusk that the tears of night began to fall, first by ones and twos, then by threes and fours, at last by fives and sixes of sevens, for the tired ones were wecking, as we weep now with them. *O! O! O! Par la pluie!*

Then there came down to the thither bank a woman of no appearance (I believe she was a Black with chills at her feet) and she gathered up his hoariness the Mookse motamourfully where he was spread and carried him away to her invisible dwelling, thats hights, *Aquila Rapax*, for he was the holy sacred solem and poshup spit of her boshop's apron. So you see the Mookse he had reason as I knew and you knew and he knew all along. And there came down to the hither bank a woman to all important (though they say that she was comely, spite the cold in her heed) and, for he was as like it as blow it to a hawker's hank, she plucked down the Gripes, torn panicky auto-tone, in angeu from his limb and cariad away its beoti-tubes with her to her unseen shieling, it is, *De Rore Coeli*. And so the poor Gripes got wrong; for that is always how a Gripes is, always was and always will be. And it was never so thoughtful of either of them. And there were left now an only elmtree and but a stone. Polled with pietrous, Sierre but saule. O! Yes! And Nuvoletta, a lass.

Then Nuvoletta reflected for the last time in her little long life and she made up all her myriads of drifting minds in one. She cancelled all her engauzements. She climbed over the bannistars; she gave a childy cloudy cry: *Nuée! Nuée!* A lightdress fluttered. She was gone. And into the river that had been a stream (for a thousand of tears had gone eon her and come on her and she was stout and struck on dancing and her muddied name was Missis-liffi) there fell a tear, a singult tear, the loveliest of all tears (I mean for those crylove fables fans who are 'keen' on the pretty-pretty commonface sort of thing you meet by hopeharrods) for it was a leaptear. But the river tripped on her by and by, lapping as though her heart was brook: *Why, why, why! Weh, O weh! I'se so silly to be flowing but I no canna stay!*

—JAMES JOYCE   *(from Finnegans Wake)*

Fables juxtaposed to display various aspects of fabulous animals

Wolf Robbed

Once a wolf was carrying home a sheep which he had plundered from the midst of a flock, when a lion met him and took it away from him. Standing at a safe distance, the wolf bawled out: "You're unjust! You've robbed me of property that was mine." The lion was delighted with this and said to the wolf in mockery: "No doubt you came by it honestly, as a present given by friends."

—BABRIUS

translated by Ben Edwin Perry

The Wolf, the Mother and the Child

A peasant's house was just outside the village,
    and the wolf lay in hiding at the door;
he had seen all sorts of prey come out—
lambs, calves and kids, a flock of turkeys,
one good meal after another, so to speak.
Yet the thief was beginning to weary of his vigil
when he heard a child crying: whereupon
the mother petted, punished, threatened him,
if he did not stop, to feed him to the wolf.
The animal made himself ready, giving thanks
to the gods for such a windfall, when the mother,
calming her beloved offspring, comforted him thus:
"Don't cry—if the wolf comes, we'll kill him."
"What's this?" exclaimed the beast, "first fair,
then foul—is that a way to treat a beast like me?
What kind of fool do they take me for? One day
the brat will come into the woods for hickory-nuts . . ."
Even as he spoke these words, a watch-dog burst
out of the house and caught him by the throat.
Pikes and pitchforks soon hemmed him in:
"What are you hanging around here for?" and
he was foolish enough to explain his reasons.
"Mercy!" the mother exclaimed, "you would eat
my boy? Do you suppose I brought him into the world
to fill the belly of the likes of you?" They killed
the poor creature then and there, one villager
cut off his head and his right front paw:

the master of the village nailed them to his door,
and these words were inscribed around the trophies:

It is a wise wolf that never hears
A mother scolding her child in tears.

—LA FONTAINE
translated by Richard Howard

The Fable of the Wulf and of the Lambe

Of the Innocent and of the shrewe Esope reherceth to vs suche a fable/ how it was so/ that the lambe and the wulf had bothe thurst/ and went bothe to a Ryuer for to drynke/ ¶It happed that the wulf dranke aboue & the lambe dranke bynethe/ And as the wulf sawe and perceyued the lambe/ he sayd with a hyghe voys/ Ha knaue why hast thou troubled and fowled my water/ whiche I shold now drynke/ Allas my lord sauf your grece/ For the water cometh fro yow toward me/ Thenne sayd the wulf to the lambe/ Hast thow no shame ne drede to curse me/ And the lambe sayd My lord with your leue/ And the wulf sayd ageyne/ Hit is not syxe monethes passyd that thy fader dyd to me as moche/ And the lambe ansuerd yet was I not at that time born/ And the wulf said ageyne to hym/ Thou hast ete my fader/ And the lambe ansuerd/ I haue no teeth/ Thenne said the wulf/ thou arte wel lyke thy fader/ and for his synne & mysdede thow shalt deye/ The wulf thenne toke the lambe and ete hym/ This fable sheweth that the euylle man retcheth not by what maner he may robbe & destroye the good & innocent man.

—WILLIAM CAXTON

The Cat and the Nightingale

A cat caught a nightingale. She buried her claws into the poor thing; and sweetly pressing tighter, said:

"My little nightingale, my darling! Everywhere you are praised for your songs, and I hear you are peered with the very best singers. Your voice—as rumored by uncle fox—is so hauntingly clear that shepherds and shepherdesses are reduced to distraction by your magical tunes. I, too, crave to hear them.

"Don't tremble, sweet, don't be stubborn. No, don't be afraid. It's not a feast I want you for. Just sing to me, anything. And then I'll let you free to dart through forests and copsewoods again. I value music the same as you: often, just purring, I put myself to sleep."

Meanwhile the poor bird could hardly breathe in the taloned grip.

"Well—come on," continued the cat. "Get something sung, my friend, even a sampling."

But the songster did not sing. He only squeaked.

"So this is what you thrilled the forests with!" the cat mocked. "Where is that purity and resonance they insist you possess? This sort of mewing I hear enough from my kittens. No. I see that at trilling you are totally artless. There's not even a proper end—or beginning. Perhaps on my tooth, then, I can savor you."

And she ate the poor song-bird to the last small bone.

—IVAN KRYLOV
translated by Martin Lopez-Morillas and Karen Kennerly

The Wolf and the Fox

Why is it that Aesop always grants the fox
superiority in wiliness?
Though I rack my brains, I cannot think why.
The wolf, when it comes to saving his skin
or seizing someone else's, knows as much—
in fact, knows more, I think; with some justice
I might dare, some time, to contradict my master.
Here, however, is a case where honors go
to the red-tailed. One night he saw
the moon reflected at the bottom of a well,
and mistook the round white shape for a cheese.
Two buckets, in turn, drew the water up:
our fox, driven by his hunger's fiercest pangs,
jumped into the bucket at the brink,
and down he went (the other bucket rose)
and only too late discovered his mistake.
How to escape, unless some other beast,
a prey to hunger and to the same delusion,
were to take the same course and rescue *him*?
Two days went by, no one came to the well,
and meanwhile unrelenting time had pared
the round face of the moon—no time to lose!
Down in the well, the fox was desperate.
Friend wolf passed by, famished as usual,
and heard himself addressed from underground:
"I have a treat for you: look what's here!
A splendid cheese that Faunus himself has made
from milk the heifer Io furnished him.

An ailing Jupiter would be cured at once
if he even tasted such a delicacy!
I've eaten this sliver already, the rest
is more than enough for you—come down
in the bucket I've left up *there* for you."
Though he tried to turn the tale to his taste,
the wolf was, plainly, a fool to believe it:
his bucket sank, his weight raised the other,
and Master Fox was hoisted up and away.

Who has the right to laugh? We let ourselves
be fooled on just as flimsy evidence.
How easy it is for each of us to believe
whatever he dreads, whatever he desires.

—LA FONTAINE
translated by Richard Howard

Fox on the Way to Mecca

On a day of days a fox was going on his pilgrimage to Mecca. As he went a cock saw him and said, "Let me ride behind you on this reed." The fox refused him, saying, "The way is long, and you cannot endure." But the cock begged him, and the fox took him up with him, and together they went. As they were on their way to Mecca, they passed a hen, which said, "Take me with you," and they took her. A little after they saw a partridge, which said to them, "Take me with you," and he rode behind the hen, and they went all four together. At the sunset they saw a cave, in which they might lodge, and the fox said to them, "Let us spend a night here, and in the morning let us go on our way." And so they did.

At night the fox watched to see where the others were going to sleep, and when all was quiet he rose up and seized upon the hen. Then hen cried out, "O my friend, what is my fault?" And he said to her "You lay eggs during the fast so that people eat and do sin." And he tore her to pieces and devoured her.

Next he caught the cock, who cried out and said to him, "And I, what have I done?" He said to him, "You wake and begin to crow before dawn, and people rise up and journey. Then thieves come and take their things." He ate him up, and then at last he caught the partridge and said to him, "And you, your sin is that you stand on a rock and make a noise for the other partridges to come to you. Then hunters come and catch them, and you fly away." And the partridge answered him and said, "Have not you eaten the hen and the cock, without giving thanks to God?" Then the fox opened his mouth, and said, "I thank God," and the partridge escaped out and flew to a rock nearby. And whenever the fox tried to approach her she flew further and further away.

—T. E. Lawrence
as adapted from an Arabian tale

The Raccoon and the Crawfish, II

The Raccoon lay by the water's edge, playing dead. Some plump Crawfish came and felt him all over. Suddenly he leapt up and devoured them. Just when he thought he had finished, he noticed two little ones he had overlooked. The larger was carrying the other on its back. When they saw him watching, they stopped and began to weep: "Please Raccoon, eat us too!"

"Oh, no." He yawned. "You are too small."

—PLAINS OJIBWA   (*Wisconsin*)

A Fayr Parable of the Foxe and the Wulf

My lord said dame Erswyn I pray you here how he can blowe with alle wyndes/ And how fayr bryngeth he his maters forth/ Thus hath he brought me many tyme in scathe & hurte said the wulf; he hath once bytrayed me to the she ape myn aunte/ Where I was in grete drede and fere, for I lefte there almost myn one ere/ Yf the foxe wil telle it how it byfel, I wyl gyve hym the fordele therof, for I can not telle it so wel but he shal beryspe me.

Wel said the foxe I shal telle it wythout stameryng. I shal saye the trouth, I pray yow herken me/ He cam in to the wode and complayned to me, that he had grete hongre/ for I sawe hym never so ful, but he wold alway have had fayne more/ I have wonder where the mete becometh that he destroyeth/ I see now on his contenonce that he begynneth to grymme for hongry. Whan I herde hym so complayne I had pyte of him, And I saide I was also hongry/ Thenne wente we half a day to gydre and fond nothyng, tho whyned he & cryted/ & said he myght goo no ferther. Thenne espyed I a grete hool standynge in the myddys under an hawe whiche was thyck of brembles, and I herde a russhyng therin. I wist not what it was, thenne said I goo therin ande loke yf ther be ony thyng ther for us/ I wote wel there is somwhat, tho said he cosyn I wolde not crape in to that hole for twenty pound but I wist fyrst what is therin, me thynketh that ther is some perylous thyng but I shal abyde here under this tree/ if ye will goo therin to fore, but come anon agayn, ande late me wete what thynge is therin/ Ye can many a subtylte and can wel helpe your self and moche better than I. See my lord the kynge, Thus he hade me poure wight to goo to fore in to the daunger, and he whiche is grete longe & stronge abode withoute and rested hym in pees/ awayte yf I dyde not for hym there.

Wold not suffre the drede and fere that I there suffred for al the good in erthe/ but yf I wyste how to escape, I wente hardyly in, I fonde the way derke, longe and brood/ Er I right in the hool cam soo espyed I a grete light whiche cam in fro that one syde there laye [in] a grete ape with tweyne grete wyde eyen/ & they glymmed as a fyre, And she had a grete mouth with longe teeth & sharp naylles on hir feet and on hir handes/ I wende hit had be a mermoyse, a baubyn or a mercatte, for I sawe never fowler beest, and by her laye thre of her children whiche were right fowle for they were ryght lyke the moder. Whan they sawe me come/ they gapeden wyd on me and were al stylle/ I was aferd/ And wold wel I had ben thens, but I thoughte I am therin/ I muste ther thurgh and come out as wel as I maye/ as I sawe her me thought she semed more than Ysegrym the wulf, and her chyldren were more than I/ I sawe never a fowler meyne/ they laye on fowle heye whiche was al be pyssed/ They were byslabbed and byclagged to their eres to in ther owen donge/ hit stanke that I was almost smoldred therof. I durst not saye but good and thenne I saide/ Aunte God gyve yow good daye and alle my cosyns your

fayr chyldren/ they be of theyr age the fayrest that ever
I sawe O lord god how wel plese they me/ how lovely/
how fayr ben they eche of them for their beaute myght
be a grete kyngis sone, Of right we ought to thanke yow,
that ye thus encrece oure lygnage/ Dere aunte whan I
herde saye that ye were delyverd and leyd doun I coude
no lenger abyde but muste come and frendly vysite yow,
I am sory that I had not erst knowen it, Reynard cosyn
said she ye be welcome, For that ye have founde me and
thus come see me I thanke yow, Dere cosyn ye be right
trewe and named right wyse in alle londes, and also that
ye gladly furthre and brynge your lignage in grete wor-
ship/ Ye muste teche my chyldren with the youris som
wysedom that they may knowe what they shal doo & leve.
I have thought on yow/ for gladly ye goo and felawship
with the good/ O how wel was I plesyd whan I herde thise
wordes/ this deservyd I at the begynnyng whan I callyd
her aunte, how be it that she was nothyng sybbe to me/
for my right aunte rukenawe that yonder standeth/
Whiche is woned to brynge forth wyse chyldren/ I saide
aunte my lyf and my good is at your commandement and
what I may doo for yow by nyght and by daye, I wylle
gladly teche them alle that I can. I wolde fayn have be
thens for the stenche of them, and also I had pyte of the
grete hongre that Isegrym had. I saide aunte I shal
comytte yow and your chyldren to god and take my leve,
My wyf shal thynke longe after me/ Dere cosyn said she
ye shal not departe til ye have eten, for yf ye dyde I wold
saie ye were not kynde. tho stode she up and brought me
in an other hool where as was moche mete of hertes &
hyndes/ was/ fesaunts, partrychs and moche other veny-

son that I wondred for whens al this mete myght come, And whan I had eten my bely ful she gaf me a grete pece of an hynde fro to ete wyth my wyf and wyth my household, whan I come home/ I was a shamed to take it/ But I myght none other wyse doo. I thankyd her & take my leve/ she bad me I shold cone sone agayn/ I sayd I wolde/ And so departed thens meryly, that I so wel had spedde, I hasted me out, & whan I cam and saw Ysegrym which laye gronyng, And I espyed hym how he ferde, he said nevew al evyll for it is wonder that I lyve/ brynge ye ony mete to ete I deye for honger. tho had I compassion of hym and gaf hym that I had. And saved hym there his lyf. wherof thenne he thanked me gretly. how be it that he now oweth me evyl wyl.

He had eten this up anon, tho said he Reynard dere cosyn what fonde ye in that hool, I am more hongry now than I was to fore my teeth ben now sharped to ete I said thenne, Eme haste yow thenne lyghtly in to that hool Ye shal fynde there ynough there lieth myn aunte wyth her chyldren if ye wyl spare the trouth and lye grete lesynges ye shal have there al your desire But & ye saye trouth ye shal take harme/ My lord was not this ynough sayd and warned who so wold understonde it that al that he fonde he shold saye the contrarye But rude and plompe beestis can not understonde wysedom therefore hate they alle subtyl Invencions/ for they can not conceyve them Yet nevertheles, he saide he wolde goo inne/ and lye so many lesynges er he sholde myshappe that all man sholde have wondre of it and so wente forth in to that fowle stynkyng hool and fonde the marmosette She was lyke

the devyls doughter and on her chyldren hynge moche
fylth cloterd in gobettis Tho cryde he alas me growleth
of thyse fowle nyckers, Come they out of helle men may
make devylles aferd of them goo and drowne them that
evyl mote they fare I sawe never fowler wormes they make
al myn heer to stande right up, Sir Ysegrym said she
what may I doo therto they ben my chyldren And I muste
be their moder What lyeth that in your weye whether
they be fowl or fayr They have yow nothyng coste here
hath ben one to day byfore yow whiche was to them
nyhe of kyn And was your getter and wyser and he sayde
that they ware fayr Who hath sente yow hyther with thyse
tydynges/ dame wyl ye wytte I wylle ete of your mete hit
is better bestowed on me than on thyse fowle wyghtes
She sayde hier is no mete/ he saide here is ynough And
there wyth he sterte with his hede toward the mete &
wolde have goon in to the hool wher the mete was. But
myn aunte sterte up wyth her chyldren and ranne to
hym wyth their sharp longe nayles so sore that the blode
ran over his eyen/ I herde hym crye sore and howle, but
I knowe of no defence that he made/ But that he ran
faste out of the hool And he was there cratched and
byten and many an hool had they made in his cote and
skyn his visage was alle on a blood, and almost he had
loste his one ere/ he groned and complayned to me sore
thene asked I hym yp he had wel lyed he sayd I saide lyke
as I sawe & fonde, and that was a fowle bytche wyth many
fowle wyghtis/ Nay eme said I, ye shold have said fayr
nece how fare ye and your fayr chyldren whiche ben my
welbelovid cosyns the wulf sayd I had lever that they
were hanged er I that saide ye eme therfore muste ye
resseyve suche maner payment, hit is better otherwhile

to lye than to saye trouthe They that ben better/ wyser
and strenger than we be have doon so to fore us See my
lord the kyng thus gate he his rede coyf/ Now stondeth
he also symply as he knewe no harme I pray yow aske ye
hym yf it was not thus/ he was not fer of yp I wote it wel.

—WILLIAM CAXTON   (*from Reynard the Foxe*)

The Donkey and the Jackal

There was once a lion named Fierce-Mane, who lived in a part of a forest. And for servant he had a jackal, a faithful drudge named Dusty.

Now one day the lion fought with an elephant, and took such cruel wounds on his body that he could not stir a foot. And since the master could not stir, Dusty grew feeble, for his throat was pinched by hunger. Then he said to the lion: "O King, I am tortured with hunger until I cannot drag one foot after another. So how can I serve you?" "My good Dusty," said the lion, "hunt out some animal that I can kill even in my present state."

So the jackal went hunting, and dragging himself to a nearby village, he saw beside a tank a donkey named Flop-Ear who was choking over the thin and prickly grass. And he drew near and said: "Uncle, my respects to you. It is long since we met. How have you grown so feeble?"

And Flop-Ear answered: "What am I to do, nephew? The laundryman is merciless, and tortures me with dreadful burdens. And he never gives me a handful of fodder. I eat nothing but this prickly grass flavored with dust, and I do not thrive."

"Well, uncle," said the jackal, "I know a lovely spot by a river, all covered with emerald grass. Come there and live with me. I promise you the pleasure of witty conversation."

"Very well said, nephew," answered Flop-Ear, "but village beasts are likely to be killed by forest animals. So what good is your charming spot to me?"

"No, no," said the jackal. "My paws form a cage to protect the spot, and no stranger has entrance there. Besides, there are three unmarried she-donkeys who were tormented just like you by laundrymen. They have now grown plump; they are young and frisky; they said to me: 'Uncle dear, go to some village and bring us a proper husband.' That is why I came to fetch you."

Now when he heard the jackal's words, Flop-Ear felt his limbs quiver with love, and he said: "In that case, my dear sir, lead the way. We will hurry there." For the poet hits the mark when he says:

> You are our only nectar; you,
> O woman, are our poison, too.
> For union with you is the breath
> Of life; and absence from you, death.

So the poor creature went with the jackal into the lion's presence. But the lion was dreadfully foolish. When he saw the donkey actually within range of his spring, he was so overjoyed that he jumped over him and landed on the other side. And the donkey wondered: "What, oh, what can this be?" For to him it seemed like the fall of a thunderbolt. Yet somehow—for fate was kind to him—he escaped quite unhurt. But when he looked back, he saw the egregious creature, cruel, horrifying, with bloodshot eyes, and he beat a hasty, terrified retreat to his own city.

Then the jackal said: "Have your spring prepared next time. For I am going to bring him to you again."

"My dear fellow," said the lion, "he saw me face to face and escaped. How can he be enticed here again? Bring me some other animal."

But the jackal said: "Why should you worry about that? I am wide awake on that point." So the jackal followed the donkey's tracks, and found him grazing in the old place.

Now when he saw the jackal, the donkey said: "Well, nephew, it was a charming spot you took me to. I was lucky to escape with my life. Tell me, what was that horrible creature? He was a thunderbolt, but he missed me."

Then the jackal laughed and said: "Uncle, that was a she-donkey. She was unspeakably lovesick, and seeing you, she rose up passionately to embrace you. But you were shy, and ran away. And as you disappeared, she stretched out a hand to detain you. That is the whole story. So come back. She has resolved to starve to death for your sake, and she says: 'If Flop-Ear does not marry me, I will plunge into fire or water, or will eat poison. Anyhow, I cannot bear to be separated from him.' So have mercy, and return. If not, you will be a woman-murderer, and the god of love will be angry. For you know:

> Woman is Love's victorious seal,
> Confers all good. If for their weal
> (Supposed) in heaven or for salvation
> Dull men hold her in detestation,
> Love strikes them for their sins forlorn,
> And some turn naked monks, some shorn;
> Some have red garments; others wear
> Skull-necklaces, or frowsy hair."

So the donkey, persuaded by this reasoning, started off with him once more. Indeed, the proverb is right:

> Men, knowing better, oft commit
>> A shabby deed—so strong is fate.
> But where are they who relish it,
>> When once it is irrevocate?

Thereupon the donkey, deceived by a hundred arguments of the rascal, came again into the presence, and was straightway killed by the lion, who had prepared his spring beforehand. And then the lion set the jackal on guard, and went himself to the river to bathe. Whereupon the greedy jackal ate the donkey's ears and heart. Now when the lion returned after bathing and repeating the proper prayers, he found the donkey minus ears and heart, and his soul was suffused with wrath, and he said to the jackal: "You scoundrel! What is this unseemly deed? You have eaten ears and heart, and my share is your leavings."

"O King," said the jackal respectfully, "do not speak so. This creature was born without ears and heart. Otherwise, how could he have come here, have seen you with his own eyes, have run in terror, and then come back? Why, it goes into poetry:

> He came, he saw, he fled
> From your appearance dread,
> Returned, forgot his fears—
> The fool lacked heart and ears."

So the lion was convinced by the jackal's argument, divided with him, and ate his own share without suspicion.

—from *The Panchatantra*
translated by Arthur W. Ryder

Birds, Beasts and Bat

Not too long ago one of the higher-ups among the hawks spotted a succulent fish in a stream far below him, and began his dive for it. He had been flying high, for by the time he got there, a bear had the fish hooked on one paw and was about to take a bite. "Get your dumb paws off that fish," screeched the hawk, "it's mine." "You must be kidding," said the bear, and with one swipe of his free paw he broke the hawk's right wing. The hawk limped off through the brush, cursing and screaming. He gathered his friends, and the bear gathered his friends, and before anybody realized what was happening, a full scale war between the birds and the beasts had begun. Every creature in the world took side, except for one.

"I figure it this way," said the Bat to himself: "I'll see which side looks like it'll come out on top, and join that one." He knew that with his leathery wings he could easily pass for a bird, and with his ears and claws he could pass for a beast.

Bat made himself a tricky reversible soldier's uniform, with bird insignia on one side and beast insignia on the other. When the beasts looked as if they would wipe out the bird forces, Bat turned his uniform beast-side and joined them, screaming, "God is on our side" and "Liberate the air!" He killed all the tiny birds he could find. When the birds had the upper hand, Bat went home, reversed his uniform, and flew back into the fray crying, "God is on our side" and "Liberate the land!" He killed all the mice and other little animals he could find.

The war went on for many months. At last the beasts and birds, tired of fighting, decided to make peace. Both sides wrote and signed many complicated treaties and documents, and set up commissions and organizations to make sure there would never be another war. Despite all the promises, there were other wars anyway; but whether they were at peace or war, from that time on neither side would have Bat.

"You fought for the beasts," screamed the Eagle, "so you must be one. Go live with your friends."

"You were on the side of the birds," roared the Lion, "so of course, you are a bird. Go live with them."

After all this, Bat became so confused and unhappy that he himself no longer knew if he was bird, beast, or anything at all. From that time until today, rejected by all sides, he has sneaked around at night, and lived in dank caves and old barns. He can fly like a bird, but he never sits in trees. Nobody knows exactly what kind of creature he is, and nobody cares.

—LEONARD JENKIN

Ape, Glow-Worm, and Bird

In a certain forest-region there was a herd of apes. And once upon a time in the winter-season, when they were suffering from cold and in great distress, they saw a glow-worm and took it for fire. They covered it over with dry sticks, grass, and leaves which they gathered, and stretched out their arms, and rubbed their arm-pits, bellies, and chests, and actually felt the comfort of imaginary warmth. Then one ape among them, who was especially chilly, kept blowing upon it all the time with his lips, giving his whole attention to it. Now a bird named Needle-beak saw this, and flew down from a tree and said: "Friend, do not trouble yourself, this is no fire, it is a glow-worm." But the other gave no heed to his words and went on blowing. And though he tried over and over again to stop him, he would not stop. To make a long story short, the bird kept coming close to his ear and nagging at him insistently, until at last the ape was enraged; and seizing him violently, smote him against a stone and killed him.

—from *The Panchatantra*
translated by Franklin Edgarton

An Ape Judge Betwixt a Fox and a Wolf

A Wolf charges a *Fox* with a piece of Pilfery. The *Fox* Denies it. The *Ape* tryes the Cause, and upon a fair Hearing, Pronounces them both to be Guilty. You (says the Judge to the *Wolf*) have the Face to challenge that which you never Lost; and you (says he to the *Fox*) have the Confidence to Deny that which you have certainly Stoll'n.

—ROGER L'ESTRANGE

Gnat and the Bull

After a gnat had settled on the curved horn of a bull he said, "Brother, have I been a burden? If I'm weighing down your neck and bending it, I will go away, over there by the pond." Said the bull, "I was not aware that you had settled on me. And if you have left, well, I didn't notice your departure either."

—Composite text of a Babylonian fable and Babrius' adaptation of the same fable

both from translations by Ben Edwin Perry

How the Pompous Remark of the Turtle Spoiled the Last Moments of the Lion Who Was Shot by a Hunter but Was Still Proud and Lonely

To return small people with pretensions to greatness to their normal size, my father tells the story of the lion wounded by the bullet of a hunter, roaring with pain and on the verge of coming to death. Came the small slow-moving turtle to the lion and said, What is your pain?

I have been shot by a hunter, the lion said.

The turtle became angry and said, May the arms of such men be broken who come to injure magnificent creatures of the earth like us.

Brother turtle, the lion said, let me tell you the injury of the hunter pains me less than what you have just said. And then the lion died.

—WILLIAM SAROYAN *(from an old Armenian fable)*

An Eagle and a Daw

An *Eagle* made a stoop at a Lamb; Truss'd it, and took it Cleverly away with her. A Mimical Daw, that saw the Exploit, would needs try the same Experiment upon a Ram: But his Claws were so shackled in the Fleece with Lugging to get him up, that the Shepherd came in, and Caught him, before he could Cleare Himself; He Clipt his Wings, and carry'd him Home to his Children to Play withal. They came Gaping about him, and ask'd their Father what strange Bird that Was? Why, says he, He'll tell you Himself that he's an *Eagle*; but if You'll take My Word for't, I know him to be a *Daw*.

—ROGER L'ESTRANGE

The Ant and the Caterpillar

As an ant, of his talents superiorly vain,
Was trotting with consequence over the plain,
A worm, in his progress, remarkably slow,
Cry'd, "Bless your good worship, wherever you go?
"I hope your great mightiness won't take it ill,
"I pay my respects from an hearty good will."

With a look of contempt, and ineffable pride,
"Begone you vile reptile," his antship reply'd:
"But first—look at me—see—my limbs how complete:
"I guide all my motions with freedom and ease;
"I run back and forward, and turn when I please.
"Of nature (grown weary) thou shocking essay!
"I spurn you thus from me;—crawl out of my way."

The reptile insulted, and vex'd to the soul,
Crept onwards, and hid himself close in his hole;
But nature determin'd to end his distress,
Soon sent him abroad in a butterfly dress.

Ere long the proud ant was repassing the road,
(Fatigued from the harvest, and tugging his load)
The beau on a violet bank he beheld,
Whose vesture in glory, a monarch excell'd;
His plumage expanded!—'twas rare to behold
So lovely a mixture of purple and gold;
The ant, quite amaz'd at a figure so gay,
Bow'd low with respect, and was trudging away:

"Stop, friend," says the butterfly, "don't be surprised;
"I once was the reptile you spurn'd and despis'd;
"But now, I can mount—in the sun-beams I play,
"While you must, forever, drudge on in your way."

The MORAL: *A wretch that to-day is o'erloaded with
sorrow, May soar above those that oppressed him tomorrow.*

—CHRISTOPHER SMART

The Grasshopper and the Ant

Grasshopper, having sung her song,
    All summer long,
Was sadly unprovided-for
When the cold winds began to roar:
Not one least bite of grub or fly
Had she remembered to put by.
Therefore she hastened to descant
On famine, to her neighbor Ant,
Begging the loan of a few grains
Of wheat to ease her hunger-pains
Until the winter should be gone.
        "You shall be paid," said she, "upon
My honor as an animal,
Both interest and principal."
The Ant was not disposed to lend:
That liberal vice was not for her.
"What did you do all summer, friend?"
She asked the would-be borrower.
        "So please your worship," answered she,
"I sang and sang both night and day."
"You sang? Indeed, that pleases me.
Then dance the winter-time away."

—LA FONTAINE
translated by Richard Wilbur

🐚 Dancing out Sand

Once Rabbit and Fox went courting a King's daughter. The King said he would give her to the one who could dance sand out of a rock. Fox danced and danced, but could not draw out the sand. At last Rabbit had his turn. But before he started, he tied a bag of sand pricked with little holes to the inside of each of his trouser legs. Then he danced, and the sand flew. He said, "Oh Buh Fox! Just look, just look!" But Fox had turned away knowing that his chance was lost.

—AMERICAN FOLK   (*Elizabeth City County, Virginia*)

The Lemming and the Owl

An Owl saw a Lemming feeding just outside of his hole. He flew down and perched at the entrance, and then said to the Lemming: "Two dog-teams are coming!" This frightened the Lemming so that he came up close to the hole, pretending he would rather be eaten by the Owl. "I am very fat," he said, "and you can have a good meal. Take me! And if you wish to celebrate before eating me, I will sing while you dance." The Owl thought this an excellent idea, drew himself up, and the Lemming began to sing. As the Owl danced, he looked up to the sky and forgot about the Lemming. Hopping from side to side, he spread his legs apart—then the Lemming ran between them into his hole. The Owl called to him to come out again, saying that the dog-teams had passed by. But the Lemming stuck his head up just long enough to throw dirt into the Owl's face.

—ESKIMO

🐢 The Tortoise and the Hippo and the Elephant

The Tortoise once built himself a village. But the Hippo came and destroyed it. The Tortoise rebuilt the village, but this time the Elephant came and trampled it. A third time the Tortoise built his village and the Hippo again destroyed it. And after rebuilding it that time the Elephant trod it flat again. Then said the Tortoise: "I am certainly tired of trying to build a village."

So he took a large cable and went to the place where the Hippo lived in the river, and proposed to him: "Let you and me match our strength by pulling on this cable. If you are able to drag me towards you, then you are the victor; if I am able to drag you, then I am the victor." The Hippo accepted the challenge readily.

Then the Tortoise went to the place of the Elephant in the swamp, and challenged him: "You have molested long enough—now let us have a test of strength with this cable. If you can move me, then you are the greater; but if I can move you, then I am the greater." The Elephant consented and said, "We will do it early tomorrow morning."

As day dawned the Tortoise went to the Hippo and said, "Now, Hippo, tie this cable tightly around your body. I am going; as soon as you feel me tug a little, pull with all your might." Then the Tortoise hurried to where the Elephant was and said, "Now, knot this cable firmly around your body; when you feel me tug a little, then you must pull with all your might."

The Tortoise crawled to where the middle of the cable lay still slack on the ground, and gave little tugs with his teeth. The Hippo thought, "So indeed the Tortoise is starting to pull." He braced himself in the roots of a giant tree and began to pull. And the Elephant also strained backwards, his trunk hooking the base of a tree. The Tortoise sat low between them. The hoops of cable tightened around each: they bloated, then suffocated, and finally killed one another.

—Bulu   (*Kamerun, West Africa*)

Man and the Weasel

A man trapped a weasel, tied her up, and went to drown her where two rivers ran together in a dank glen. While thrashing to skim the current's surface, the weasel complained: "I keep your house clear of mice and lizards. How miserably you repay my efforts!" Said the man as he lowered her in: "True; but you do it to fill your belly, not to help me—and in the meantime devour what they would have eaten."

—adapted from BABRIUS and ROGER L'ESTRANGE

by Karen Kennerly

The Man and The Snake

A man saw a snake: "Nasty thing!"
he said, "I'll do something now
the world will thank me for . . ."
And thereupon the perverse creature
(I refer to the snake, not the man,
let no mistake be made about that),
once captured, was thrust into a sack
and, worse still, condemned to death,
whether guilty or quite blameless.
In order to make some show of reason,
however, the man uttered this speech:
"Symbol of ingratitude! to grant mercy
to the wicked is to be a fool: die!
Your fury and your fangs will never
do me harm." The snake, in its tongue,
replied as best it could, "If all
the ungrateful in the world were to be
punished, who should get off free?
You judge yourself, and I merely follow
your example: you have only to look at yourself.
My life is in your hands, take it—
your justice is your convenience,
your pleasure no more than your whim:
according to such laws, condemn me,
but my dying words will let you know
that the symbol of ingratitude is not
the serpent, to tell the truth, but man."
These words stayed the man's hand,

and he stepped back, but then returned
to the charge: "Frivolous reasoning:
the decision is mine by right—still,
let us seek counsel elsewhere." "Let us,"
the serpent replied. A cow was nearby,
was summoned, and joined the pair.
The case was set forth, and judged:
"What need was there to disturb me?
The snake is right—why conceal it?
Year after year I have fed this man;
without me, he would not have lived a day;
he takes it all for himself—my milk,
my calves, and lives thereby in comfort—
I have even restored his health when age
and time ravaged them, and my efforts
are given over to his pleasure as well
as to his needs. Now I am old myself,
and he leaves me in a barren pen!
If only I could graze at will, but no,
I am tied here, and were the snake my master,
could ingratitude be carried further?
Enough, I have said what I think."
The man, astounded by such arbitration,
said to the snake: "Don't believe a word!
The senile creature has lost her wits.
Let us consult, instead, one of my oxen."
"Let us, indeed," the serpent agreed.
No sooner said than done. Slowly the ox
approached, and having ruminated the case,
delivered himself of this judgment:
For long and laborious years, he had borne
the weight of wearisome tasks, dragging
from the fields to the barns those harvests

Ceres gives so cheaply to men, and sells
so dear to beasts of burden. And for reward,
had received, for all his toil, many blows
but few thanks; then, grown old, he was
supposed to be honored to supply his blood
whereby men buy the favor of the gods!
So spoke the ox, whereupon the man replied,
"Enough of this tiresome rhetoric!
The creature puts on airs by coming
among us not as a judge but a prosecutor.
I dismiss his testimony as well." The tree
was then consulted, but with worse results:
having served as a refuge against heat,
rain, and all the fury of the winds as well,
having embellished man's gardens and his fields,
shade was not the only benefit provided,
for did not each branch bend with fruit?
Yet in payment, a peasant with an axe
chopped it down—so much for wages, though
the year round it gave blossoms in spring,
fruit in autumn, shade in summer, in winter
the joys of the hearth. Could it not be pruned,
rather than suffer such drastic treatment?
By nature, indeed, it would have been living still.
Refusing to be convinced, the man then sought
To win his case at all costs: "What good,"
he muttered, "listening to such counsel!"
and flung the sack so hard against the walls
that he soon disposed of the snake inside it.

Thus the great behave: reason offends them,
they assume that all exists for their sake,

animals and men alike, and serpents too.
If anyone tries to protest, he is a fool.
With which I agree, but what is one to do?
Speak at a distance, or else hold one's tongue.

—La Fontaine
translated by Richard Howard

Various oral and literary modes which narrate fables

*That which is Aesopic is confined to instructive examples,
nor is anything else aimed at in fables, except that the mis-
takes of mortals may be corrected, and that one may sharpen
his wits by a close application to them. . . I shall indeed take
care to preserve the spirit of the famous old man; but if I
chose to insert something of my own, for a variety of expression, I would have you, reader, accept it in good faith, provided that my brevity be a suitable recompense for taking
that liberty.*

—PHAEDRUS

The Fox and the Stork

I t is not right to injure any man; but if someone does
inflict an injury, this fable warns him that he is liable
to punishment in kind.

A fox is said to have invited a stork to dinner and to
have set before her on a slab of marble some thin soup,
which the stork, though hungry, could find no way to
taste. Then the stork in turn invited the fox to dinner
and set before him a narrow-mouthed jar full of solid
food, into which she thrust her beak and so satisfied her
own appetite while tormenting her guest with hunger.
As the fox was vainly licking the neck of the jar the pilgrim bird, so we have heard, made this remark: "One
who sets an example ought to bear it with patience when
he gets the same in return."

—PHAEDRUS
translated by Ben Edwin Perry

There will not be found in [my fables] either the elegance or extreme brevity which characterizes Phaedrus; these qualities are beyond my reach. As it was out of my power to imitate him in these points, I thought that I ought in return to ornament my productions more than he had done. For the constraints of poetry, joined to the severity of our own language, in many places embarrassed me, and banished that simplicity which one may well call the soul of the Fable, since in its absence it necessarily languishes.

—LA FONTAINE

The Fox and the Turkeys

Against the assaults of a hungry fox,
 some turkeys took to the branches of a tree,
their citadel. The wily creature circled
the trunk, gazing up at the vigilant birds.
"What!" he exclaimed, "they dare flout me,
as if they alone were exempt from the common law—
no, by all the gods, no!" Which was all he had to say.
The moon came out, and seemed, despite the fox,
to favor the strategy adopted by the fowls.
The fox, a novice in matters of siege,
resorted to all his cunning tricks: pretended
trying to climb the tree, leaping into the air,
falling back, playing dead, then reviving—
Harlequin himself could not have played so many
parts: he raised his tail, made it gleam

164:

like a torch, and executed a thousand other
maneuvers, during which no turkey dared to sleep.
Their foe exhausted them by keeping their eyes
fixed on the same object, without a moment's peace.
The poor creatures were ultimately stupefied,
falling one after the next: no sooner caught
than killed and kept aside; nearly half the flock
succumbed. The fox carried them to his larder.

Paying too much attention to peril more often
than not claims the same victims as the danger.

—LA FONTAINE

translated by Richard Howard

In the first place [a fable] should have only one moral; sec-ondly, the various parts should be so constructed that their general purpose and connection be at once apparent; thirdly, every one of these parts should form a particular whole, and constitute a fable in itself, so that the general fable should be homogeneous . . . each part appealing to *an individual per-ception, and all of them together illustrating a general one. . . . its highest ornament is to have no ornament at all.*

—G. E. LESSING

The Ass and the Fox

Tell me of any animal I cannot imitate," boasted the Ass to the Fox. "And you," the Fox returned, "tell me of one who would by chance imitate you."

My fellow authors, need I explain myself further?

—G. E. LESSING
translated by James Burns

Spoken narratives are events, not just verbal descriptions of events. If one listens not only for meaning but for sounds and for intervening silences, it becomes clear that what has been read as a kind of "oral prose" is in reality dramatic poetry.

—DENNIS TEDLOCK

At Gourd-Patch Rise Old Lady Junco Had Her Home and Coyote

Coyote was staying there at Sitting Rock with his
    children.
(He was with his children)
and Old Lady Junco
was winnowing.
She was winnowing pigweed
and tumbleweed seeds.
(With her basket)
she winnowed these by tossing them in the air.
(She was tossing them in the air) and meanwhile Coyote
Coyote
was going around hunting, hunting to feed his children
when he came to where Junco was winnowing.
"What are you doing?" that's what he said. "Well, I'm
    winnowing."
"What are you winnowing?" "Well

pigweed and tumbleweed" (that's what she said). "Indeed.
What are you singing?" "Well, this is my winnowing
song."
"Now SING IT for me
so that I
may sing it for my children."
Old Lady Junco sang
for Coyote:

                    H I N A   H I N A
        Y U U W A   Y U U W A

                    H I N A   H I N A
        Y U U W A   Y U U W A

                    H I N A   H I N A
            Y U   Y U

(*blowing*)   PFFFF PFFFF

                    H I N A   H I N A
        Y U   Y U

(*blowing*)   PFFFF PFFFF

That's what she sang.
"WELL NOW
I can go and sing it to my children."
Coyote went on, and when he came to Angleworm Arroyo

168:

MOURNING DOVES FLEW UP!
and he lost his song.
He went back.
(*mumbling*) "Quick! When some mourning doves flew up
I lost my song."
Again she sang for him.
He learned the song and went on.
Going through a field
he broke through a gopher hole there.
Again he lost his song.
Again, for the third time
he asked for it.
Again she sang for him.
When he came to Angleworm Arroyo for the third time
BLACKBIRDS FLEW UP! and again he lost his song.
(He was coming for the fourth time
and Old Lady Junco said to herself, (*mumbling*) "Here
        you come
but I won't sing," she said.
She looked for a round rock.)
She found a round rock, and she
dressed the rock with her Junco shirt and put her basket
        of seeds with it.
(*mumbling*) ("As for you, you may do whatever you
        wish.") Junco went inside her house.
Coyote came for the fourth time.
When he came:
"Quick! Sing it for me again," he said.
Junco said nothing.
"Quick!" he said, but she didn't speak.
"ONE!
If I count

to four

and you still haven't spoken, I'll bite you," he said.

"This is the second time, TWO!
Quick! Sing for me."
She didn't sing. "THREE! I'll count ONCE MORE."

Coyote said, "QUICK! Sing," he said.
She didn't sing.
He bit the round rock
with the Junco shirt, CRUNCH! Coyote bit the stone
    Junco.
Right here (*points to molars*) he knocked them out, he
    knocked out the ones in back, the rows of teeth there.
(*mumbling*) "So! This is what I meant to do to you,"
    Junco said. "AY! AY!" he said.
HE WENT BACK TO HIS CHILDREN, and when he
    got there he found out that all his children had
    starved to death.
This was lived long ago. That's why Coyote has no teeth
    here (*points to molars*). LEEEEEE SEMKONIKYA.
    (*laughs*)

—Zuni   (*New Mexico*)
translated by Dennis Tedlock

170:

The Goat Without a Beard

T is certain that the modish passions
    Descend among the crowd, like fashions.
Excuse me, then, if pride, conceit,
(The manners of the fair and great)
I give to monkeys, asses, dogs,
Fleas, owls, goats, butterflies, and hogs.
I say that these are proud, what then?
I never said they equal men.

    A Goat (as vain as Goat can be)
Affected singularity;
Whene'er a thymy bank he found,
He roll'd upon the fragrant ground,
And then with fond attention stood,
Fix'd o'er his image in the flood.
    "I hate my frowzy beard," he cries,
"My youth is lost in this disguise.
Did not the females know my vigour,
Well might they loath this reverend figure."
    Resolved to smooth his shaggy face,
He sought the barber of the place.
A flippant monkey, spruce and smart,
Hard by, profess'd the dapper art.
His pole with pewter basins hung,
Black rotten teeth in order strung,
Ranged cups, that in the window stood,

Lined with red rags, to look like blood,
Did well his threefold trade explain,
Who shaved, drew teeth, and breathed a vein.

 The Goat he welcomes with an air,
And seats him in his wooden chair:
Mouth, nose, and cheek, the lather hides;
Light, smooth, and swift, the razor glides.

 "I hope your custom, Sir," says Pug,
"Sure never face was half so smug!"

 The Goat, impatient for applause.
Swift to the neighbouring hill withdraws;
The shaggy people grinn'd and stared,—

 —"Heyday! what's here? without a beard!
Say, brother, whence the dire disgrace?
What envious hand hath robb'd your face?"—
When thus the fop with smiles of scorn:
"Are beards by civil nations worn?—
E'en Muscovites have mow'd their chins.
Shall we, like formal Capuchins
Stubborn in pride, retain the mode,
And bear about the hairy load?
Whene'er we through the village stray,
Are we not mock'd along the way,
Insulted with loud shouts of scorn,
By boys, our beards disgraced and torn?"

 "Were you no more with Goats to dwell,
Brother, I grant you reason well;"
Replies a bearded chief. "Beside,
If boys can mortify thy pride,
How wilt thou stand the ridicule

Of our whole flock? Affected fool!
Coxcombs, distinguish'd from the rest,
To all but coxcombs are a jest."

—JOHN GAY

The Two Dogs

The dog wags his tongue at a millstone,
  And says to his companion
"It is an omen from heaven! I will put an elegant leash on
  it for you."

—SUMER
translated by Edmund Gordon

174:

*The first to tell fables to the sons of the Hellenes, they say,
was Aesop the wise . . . It remains for me to present them in
a new and poetic dress, bridling the iambic verse of my fables, like a war-horse, with trappings of gold. . . . But I tell
my fables in a transparent style. I do not sharpen the teeth
of the iambs, but I test them and refine them, as it were, in
the fire, and I am careful to soften their sting.*

—BABRIUS

Piscator's Pleasantry

A musical fisherman fancied a day's catch
        might swim ashore—no sweat—
enthralled by his dulcet fluting.
So he put away his net
and piped as though he were the Muses' match.

But when he tired of spending breath in vain,
he cast his heavy seine
and hauled it high and dry replete with fishes,
observing whose twitches
he said in banter as he washed his gear:
"No music here;
you should have danced before, while I was tooting."

Loafing and vagaries will bring no riches.
But when by toil you take what you like best,
then is the time for wasting time in jest.

—BABRIUS

translated by Robert Fitzgerald

When the King perceived that [his three sons] were hostile to education, he summoned his counselors and said, "Gentlemen, it is known to you that these sons of mine, being hostile to education, are lacking in discernment. . . . Some means must therefore be devised to awaken their intelligence.". . . One of their number, a counselor named Keen, said: "Oh King, the duration of life is limited and the verbal sciences require much time for mastery. Therefore let some kind of epitome be devised to wake their intelligence.

"Now, there is a Brahman named Vishnusharman with a reputation for competence in numerous sciences. Entrust the princes to him.

Vishnusharman took the boys and made them learn by heart five books which he composed. . . . These the princes learned, and in six months' time they answered the prescription. Since that day this work on the art of intelligent living, called Panchatantra *has traveled the world, awakening the intelligence of the young.*

—from the introduction to *The Panchatantra*

The Frogs That Rode Snakeback

There was once an elderly black snake in a certain spot, and his name was Slow-Poison. He considered the situation from this point of view: "How in the world can I get along without overtaxing my energies?" Then he went to a pond containing many frogs, and behaved as if very dejected.

As he waited thus, a frog came to the edge of the

water and asked: "Uncle, why don't you bustle about today for food as usual?"

"My dear friend," said Slow-Poison, "I am afflicted. Why should I wish for food? For this evening, as I was bustling about for food, I saw a frog and made ready to catch him. But he saw me and, fearing death, he escaped among some Brahmans intent upon holy recitation, nor did I perceive which way he went. But in the water at the edge of the pond was the great toe of a Brahman boy, and stupidly deceived by its resemblance to a frog, I bit it, and the boy died immediately. Then the sorrowing father cursed me in these terms: 'Monster! Since you bit my harmless son, you shall for this sin become a vehicle for frogs, and shall subsist on whatever they choose to allow you.' Consequently, I have come here to serve as your vehicle."

Now the frog reported this to all the others. And every last one of them, in extreme delight, went and reported to the frog-king, whose name was Water-Foot. He in turn, accompanied by his counselors, rose hurriedly from the pond—for he thought it an extraordinary occurrence—and climbed upon Slow-Poison's hood. The others also, in order of age, climbed on his back. Yet others, finding no vacant spot, hopped along behind the snake. Now Slow-Poison, with an eye to making his living, showed them fancy turns in great variety. And Water-Foot, enjoying contact with his body, said to him:

> I'd rather ride Slow-Poison than
>   The finest horse I've seen,
> Or elephant, or chariot,
>   Or man-borne palanquin.

The next day, Slow-Poison was wily enough to move very slowly. So Water-Foot said: "My dear Slow-Poison, why don't you carry us nicely, as you did before?"

And Slow-Poison said: "O King, I have no carrying power today because of lack of food." "My dear fellow," said the king, "eat the plebeian frogs."

When Slow-Poison heard this, he quivered with joy in every member and made haste to say: "Why, that is a part of the curse laid on me by the Brahman. For that reason I am greatly pleased at your command." So he ate frogs uninterruptedly, and in a very few days he grew strong. And with delight and inner laughter he said:

> The trick was good. All sorts of frogs
> Within my power have passed.
> The only question that remains,
> Is: How long will they last?

Water-Foot, for his part, was befooled by Slow-Poison's plausibilities, and did not notice a thing.

At this moment another black snake, a tremendous fellow, arrived on the scene. And being amazed at the sight of Slow-Poison used as a vehicle by frogs, he said: "Partner, they are our natural food, yet they use you as a vehicle. This is repellent." And Slow-Poison said:

> I know I should not carry frogs;
> I have it well in mind;
> But I am marking time, as did
> The Brahman butter-blind.

"How was that?" asked the snake. And Slow-Poison told the story of

The Butter-Blinded Brahman

There was once a Brahman named Theodore in a certain town. His wife, being unchaste and a pursuer of other men, was forever making cakes with sugar and butter for a lover, and so cheating her husband.

Now one day her husband saw her and said: "My dear wife, what are you cooking? And where are you forever carrying cakes? Tell the truth."

But her impudence was equal to the occasion, and she lied to her husband: "There is a shrine of the blessèd goddess not far from here. There I have undertaken a fasting ceremony, and I take an offering, including the most delicious dishes." Then she took the cakes before his very eyes and started for the shrine of the goddess, imagining that after her statement, her husband would believe it was for the goddess that his wife was daily providing delicious dishes. Having reached the shrine, she went down to the river to perform the ceremonial bath.

Meanwhile her husband arrived by another road and hid behind the statue of the goddess. And his wife entered the shrine after her bath, performed the various rites—laving, anointing, giving incense, making an offering, and so on—bowed before the goddess, and prayed: "O blessèd one, how may my husband be made blind?"

Then the Brahman behind the goddess' back spoke, disguising his natural tone: "If you never stop giving him such food as butter and butter-cakes, then he will presently go blind."

Now that loose female, deceived by the plausible revelation, gave the Brahman just that kind of food every day. One day the Brahman said: "My dear, I don't see very well." And she thought: "Thank the goddess."

Then the favored lover thought: "The Brahman has gone blind. What can he do to me?" Whereupon he came daily to the house without hesitation.

"And that is why I say:

I know I should not carry frogs . . . .

and the rest of it."

Then Slow-Poison, with noiseless laughter, hummed over the verse:

The trick was good. All sorts of frogs . . . .

and the rest of it. And Water-Foot, hearing this, was conscience stricken, and wondering what he meant, inquired: "My dear sir, what do you mean by reciting that repulsive verse?" "Nothing at all," said Slow-Poison, desiring to mask his purpose. And Water-Foot, befooled by his plausible manner, failed to perceive his treachery.

Why spin it out? He ate them all so completely that not even frog-seed was left.

"And that is why I say:

Bear even foes upon your back, ..."

—from *The Panchatantra*
translated by Arthur W. Ryder

Every fable is invented to show men what they ought to fol-
low and what they ought to flee. For fables mean as much in
poetry as words in theology. And so I shall write fables to
show the ways of good men.

—WILLIAM CAXTON

(taken from Julian Macho's French edition of Aesop's fables)

The Fable of the Ape and of His Two Children

He that somtyme men dispreysen/ may wel helpe somme other/ as hit appereth by this Fable of an Ape/ whiche had two children/ of the whiche he hated the one/ & loued the other/ whiche he toke in his armes/ and with hym fled before the dogges/ And whanne the other sawe/ that his moder lefte hym behynde/ he ranne and lepte on her back/ And by cause that the lytyl ape whiche the she ape held in her armes empeched her to flee/ she lete hit falle to the erthe/ And the other whiche the moder hated held fast and was saued/ the whiche from thens forthon kyssed and embraced his moder/ And she thenne beganne to loue hym/ wherfore many tymes it happeth/ that that thynge whiche is dispreysed/ is better than that thynge whiche is loued and preysed/ For somtyme the children whiche ben preysed and loued/ done lasse good than they whiche ben dispreysed and hated

—WILLIAM CAXTON

:181

We have had several English paraphrases upon Aesop and divers of his followers, both in prose and in verse: the latter have perchance ventured a little too far from the precise scope of the author upon the privilege of a poetical license. And for the other of ancient date, the morals are so insipid and flat, and the style and diction of the fables so coarse and uncouth, that they are rather dangerous, than profitable, as to the purpose they were intended for."

—Roger L'Estrange

The Owl and the Sun

There was a Pinking Owl once upon a very Bright and a Glorious Morning, that sate Sputtering at the *Sun*, and ask'd him what he meant to stand staring her in the *Eyes* at that *Rate*. Well, says the *Sun*, but if your *Eyes* will not bare the *Light*, what's your Quarrel to *my Beams* that *Shed* it? Do you think it a Reasonable thing that the whole World should be Deprived of the Greatest Blessing in Nature, to Gratify the Folly, the Arrogance and the Infirmity of One Sot?

The MORAL: *There is nothing so Excellent, or so Faultless, but Envy and Detraction will find somewhat to say against it.*

—Roger L'Estrange

When Brer 'Possum Attend Miss Fox's House-Party

O nce long before the war, when times was good, Miss Fox she set out for to give a house-party, Miss Fox did.

And Miss Fox she 'low she ain' going invite the lastest person to her house-party 'cepting the quality; and when Brer Fox he just mention Brer 'Possum's name, Miss Fox she rare and charge, Miss Fox do. She give it to Brer Fox, and she 'low how she don' invite no poor white trash to her house-party; and she 'low, Miss Fox do, how Brer Fox must set his mind on giving a tacky party.

Brer Fox he 'low how Brer 'Possum ain' no poor white trash; but Miss Fox she 'clare Brer 'Possum ain' no more than a half-strainer, and so Miss Fox she don' invite Brer 'Possum to her house-party.

Well, Brer 'Possum he feel mighty broke up when he hear all the other creeters talking about the house-party, 'case Brer 'Possum he have plenty money. Brer 'Possum are a mighty shifty man, and always have plenty money.

Well, Brer 'Possum he tell Brer Rabbit how he feel 'bout Miss Fox house-party; and he ax Brer Rabbit, Brer 'Possum do, why he don' be invited.

Brer Rabbit he 'low it all because Brer 'Possum don' hold up his head and wear store clothes; and Brer Rabbit he advise Brer 'Possum to order hisself some real quality clothes, and a churn hat, and go to Miss Fox house-party; and he 'low, Brer Rabbit do, how they won't know Brer

'Possum, and mistake hisself sure for some man from the city.

So old Brer 'Possum he got plenty money, and he go to the city, Brer 'Possum do; and he order just a quality suit of clothes, Brer 'Possum do; and he go to the barber, and get hisself shaved, and his hair cut, and he present hisself at Miss Fox house-party.

Well, you may be sure Brer 'Possum he receive flattering attention, he surely did; and the last one of the people asking, "Who that fine gentleman?" "Who that city gentleman?" "Who that stinguished-looking gentleman?" and Brer Rabbit he make hisself forward to introduce Brer 'Possum right and left, "My friend Mr. Potsum from Augusta!" That old Brer Rabbit he done say "Potsum," 'case enduring they find him out, that old Brer Rabbit he going swear and kiss the book he done say 'possum, all the time. That just exactly what that old man Rabbit going to do.

But, Lord bless you! they all that taken up with the fine gentleman, they don' spicion hisself; and he pass a mighty proudful evening, Brer 'Possum do.

But when it come retiring-time, and the gentlemans all get their candles, and 'scorted to their rooms, Brer 'Possum he look at the white bed, and he look all 'bout the room, and he feel powerful uncomfortable, Brer 'Possum do, 'case Brer 'Possum he never sleep in a bed in all his born days. Brer 'Possum he just can't sleep in a bed.

The poor old man he walk round the room, and round the room, twell the house get asleep; and he take off all his fine clothes, and he open the door softly, and step out all to hisself, he powerful tired; and he just climb a tree what stand by the porch, and hang hisself off by his tail and fall asleep.

In the morning, when Miss Fox get up and open the door, she see Brer 'Possum hanging from the limb. She that astonished she can't believe her eyes; but Miss Fox know a fine fat 'possum when she see him, she surely do.

Well, Miss Fox she cotch hold of Brer 'Possum and kill him, and dress him, and serve him up on the breakfast-table; and the guests they compliment Miss Fox on her fine 'Possum breakfast; but when they go call the fine gentleman from the City, they just find his fine clothes, but they never suspicion where he done gone, twell many day after, when old Brer Rabbit he done let the secret out.

—AMERICAN FOLK (*Georgia*)

Fish Dance

Because of complaints against the high judges, against the magnates, and against the rich, the Lion grew irritable: He trekked out, himself, to inspect his domains. On the way, a peasant by a new kindled fire was beginning to fry some fish he'd just caught—poor things, they tried to hop high from the heat since each knew his fate and lashed madly about.

That cavernous mouth yawned wide with shock: "Who are you?" the Lion roared, "what are you doing?" Fawningly the rustic spoke. "Mighty Tsar, I am the mayor of this watery parish; and these are the elders, deep-dwellers every one. We've all of us turned out to salute your arrival." "Well, how do they fare? Is your province abundant?" "My Lord—it's not mere existence—it's paradise! The only gift we can ask of the gods is that your own precious days be duly extended."

(While the fish in the pan incessantly thrash)

"But why," asked the Lion, "What is the reason they wag their heads and tails so queerly?" "Oh learned Tsar, the joy of seeing you makes them dance." Content with that, the Lion licked the peasant affectionately on his chest. And deigning to glimpse once more at the dance, he continued on his inspectering tour.

—Ivan Krylov
translated by Martin Lopez-Morillas and Karen Kennerly

Fables couched in other literary forms

The Cock and the Fox: Or, The Tale of the Nun's Priest, from Chaucer

L O N G   T A L E

There liv'd, as Authors tell, in Days of Yore,
   A Widow somewhat old, and very poor:
Deep in a Dell her Cottage lonely stood,
Well thatch'd, and under covert of a Wood.
      This Dowager, on whom my Tale I found,
Since last she laid her Husband in the Ground,
A simple sober Life, in patience led,
And had but just enough to buy her Bread:
But Huswifing the little Heav'n had lent,
She duly paid a Groat for Quarter-Rent;
And pinch'd her Belly with her Daughters two,
To bring the Year about with much ado.
      The Cattel in her Homestead were three Sows,
An Ewe call'd *Mally*; and three brinded Cows.
Her Parlor-Window stuck with Herbs around,
Of sav'ry Smell; and Rushes strew'd the Ground.
A Maple-Dresser, in her Hall she had,
On which full many a slender Meal she made:
For no delicious Morsel pass'd her Throat;
According to her Cloth she cut her Coat:
No paynant Sawce she knew, no costly Treat,
Her Hunger gave a Relish to her Meat:
A sparing Diet did her Health assure;

Or sick, a Pepper-Posset was her Cure.
Before the Day was done her Work she sped,
And never went by Candle-light to Bed:
With Exercise she sweat ill Humors out,
Her Dancing was not hinder'd by the Gout.
Her Poverty was glad; her Heart content,
Nor knew she what the Spleen or Vapors meant.

      Of Wine she never tasted through the Year,
But White and Black was all her homely Chear;
Brown Bread, and Milk, (but first she skim'd her Bowls)
And Rashers of sindg'd Bacon, on the Coals.
On Holy-Days, an Egg or two at most;
But her Ambition never reach'd to roast.

      A Yard she had with Pales enclos'd about,
Some high, some low, and a dry Ditch without.
Within this Homestead, liv'd without a Peer,
For crowing loud, the noble Chanticleer:
So hight her Cock, whose singing did surpass
The merry Notes of Organs at the Mass.
More certain was the crowing of a Cock
To number Hours, than is an Abbey-clock;
And sooner than the Mattin-Bell was rung,
He clap'd his Wings upon his Roost, and sung:
For when Degrees fifteen ascended right,
By sure Instinct he knew 'twas One at Night.
High was his Comb, and Coral-red withal,
In dents embattel'd like a Castle-Wall;
His Bill was Raven-black, and shon like Jet,
Blue were his Legs, and Orient were his Feet:
White were his Nails, like Silver to behold,
His Body glitt'ring like the burnish'd Gold.

This gentle Cock for solace of his Life,
Six Misses had beside his lawful Wife;
Scandal that spares no King, tho' ne'er so good,
Says, they were all of his own Flesh and Blood:
His Sisters both by Sire, and Mother's side,
And sure their likeness show'd them near ally'd.
But make the worst, the Monarch did no more,
Than all the *Ptolomeys* had done before:
When Incest is for Int'rest of a Nation,
'Tis made no Sin by Holy Dispensation.
Some Lines have been maintain'd by this alone,
Which by their common Ugliness are known.

But passing this as from our Tale apart,
Dame Partlet was the Soveraign of his Heart:
Ardent in Love, outragious in his Play,
He feather'd her a hundred times a Day:
And she that was not only passing fair,
But was withal discreet, and debonair,
Resolv'd the passive Doctrin to fulfil
Tho' loath: And let him work his wicked Will.
At Board and Bed was affable and kind,
According as their Marriage-Vow did bind,
And as the Churches Precept had enjoin'd.
Ev'n since she was a Sennight old, they say
Was chast, and humble to her dying Day,
Nor Chick nor Hen was known to disobey.

By this her Husband's Heart she did obtain,
What cannot Beauty, join'd with Virtue, gain!
She was his only Joy, and he her Pride,
She, when he walk'd, went pecking by his side;
If spurning up the Ground, he sprung a Corn,

The Tribute in his Bill to her was born.
But oh! what Joy it was to hear him sing
In Summer, when the Day began to spring,
Stretching his Neck, and warbling in his Throat,
Solus cum Sola, then was all his Note.
For in the Days of Yore, the Birds of Parts
Were bred to Speak, and Sing, and learn the lib'ral Arts.

    It happ'd that perching on the Parlor-beam
Amidst his Wives he had a deadly Dream;
Just at the Dawn, and sigh'd, and groan'd so fast,
As ev'ry Breath he drew wou'd be his last.
Dame Partlet, ever nearest to his Side,
Heard all his piteous Moan, and how he cry'd
For help from Gods and Men: And sore aghast
She peck'd and pull'd, and waken'd him at last.
Dear Heart, said she, for Love of Heav'n declare
Your Pain, and make me Partner of your Care.
You groan, Sir, ever since the Morning-light,
As something had disturb'd your noble Spright.

    And Madam, well I might, said Chanticleer,
Never was *Shrovetide*-Cock in such a fear.
Ev'n still I run all over in a Sweat,
My Princely Senses not recover'd yet.
For such a Dream I had of dire Portent,
That much I fear my Body will be shent:
It bodes I shall have Wars and woful Strife,
Or in a loathsom Dungeon end my Life.
Know Dame, I dreamt within my troubled Breast,
That in our Yard, I saw a murd'rous Beast,
That on my Body would have made Arrest.
With waking Eyes I ne'er beheld his Fellow,
His Colour was betwixt a Red and Yellow:

Tipp'd was his Tail, and both his pricking Ears
With black; and much unlike his other Hairs:
The rest, in shape a Beagle's Whelp throughout,
With broader Forehead, and a sharper Snout:
Deep in his Front were sunk his glowing Eyes,
That yet methinks I see him with Surprize.
Reach out your Hand, I drop with clammy Sweat,
And lay it to my Heart, and feel it beat.

　　　　Now fy for Shame, quoth she, by Heav'n above,
Thou hast for ever lost thy Ladies Love;
No Woman can endure a Recreant Knight,
He must be bold by Day, and free by Night:
Our Sex desires a Husband or a Friend,
Who can our Honour and his own defend;
Wise, Hardy, Secret, lib'ral of his Purse:
A Fool is nauseous, but a Coward worse:
No bragging Coxcomb, yet no baffled Knight,
How dar'st thou talk of Love, and dar'st not Fight?
How dar'st thou tell thy Dame thou art affer'd,
Hast thou no manly Heart, and hast a Beard?

　　　　If ought from fearful Dreams may be divin'd,
They signify a Cock of Dunghill-kind.
All Dreams, as in old *Gallen* I have read,
Are from Repletion and Complexion bred:
From rising Fumes of indigested Food,
And noxious Humors that infect the Blood:
And sure, my Lord, if I can read aright,
These foolish Fancies you have had to Night
Are certain Symptoms (in the canting Style)
Of boiling Choler, and abounding Bile:
This yellow Gaul that in your Stomach floats,
Ingenders all these visionary Thoughts.

When Choler overflows, then Dreams are bred
Of Flames and all the Family of Red;
Red Dragons, and red Beasts in sleep we view;
For Humors are distinguish'd by their Hue.
From hence we dream of Wars and Warlike Things,
And Wasps and Hornets with their double Wings.
   Choler adust congeals our Blood with Fear;
Then black Bulls toss us, and black Devils tear.
In sanguine airy Dreams aloft we bound,
With Rhumes oppress'd we sink in Rivers drown'd.
      More I could say, but thus conclude my Theme,
The dominating Humour makes the Dream.
Cato was in his time accounted Wise,
And he condemns them all for empty Lies.
Take my Advice, and when we fly to Ground
With Laxatives preserve your Body sound,
And purge the peccant Humors that abound.
I should be loath to lay you on a Bier;
And though there lives no 'Pothecary near,
I dare for once prescribe for your Disease,
And save long Bills, and a damn'd Doctor's Fees.
      Two Soveraign Herbs, which I by practise know,
And both at Hand, (for in our Yard they grow;)
On peril of my Soul shall rid you wholly
Of yellow Choler, and of Melancholy:
You must both Purge, and Vomit; but obey,
And for the love of Heav'n make no delay.
Since hot and dry in your Complexion join,
Beware the Sun when in a vernal Sign;
For when he mounts exalted in the Ram,
If then he finds your Body in a Flame,
Replete with Choler, I dare lay a Groat,

A Tertian Ague is at least your Lot.
Perhaps a Fever (which the Gods forefend)
May bring your Youth to some untimely end.
And therefore, Sir, as you desire to live,
A Day or two before your Laxative,
Take just three Worms, nor over nor above,
Because the Gods unequal Numbers love.
These Digestives prepare you for your Purge,
Of Fumetery, Centaury, and Spurge,
And of Ground-Ivy add a Leaf, or two,
All which within our Yard or Garden grow.
Eat these, and be, my Lord, of better Cheer,
Your Father's Son was never born to fear.

    Madam, quoth he, Grammercy for your Care,
But *Cato*, whom you quoted, you may spare:
'Tis true, a wise, and worthy Man he seems,
And (as you say) gave no belief to Dreams:
But other Men of more Authority,
And by th' Immoral Pow'rs as wise as He
Maintain, with sounder Sense, that Dreams forbode;
For *Homer* plainly says they come from God.
Nor *Cato* said it: But some modern Fool,
Impos'd in *Cato*'s Name on Boys at School.

    Believe me, Madam, Morning Dreams foreshow
Th' events of Things, and future Weal or Woe:
Some Truths are not by Reason to be try'd,
But we have sure Experience for our Guide.
An ancient Author, equal with the best,
Relates this Tale of Dreams among the rest.

    Two Friends, or Brothers, with devout Intent,
On some far Pilgrimage together went.
It happen'd so that when the Sun was down,

They just arriv'd by twilight at a Town;
That Day had been the baiting of a Bull,
'Twas at a Feast, and ev'ry Inn so full;
That no void Room in Chamber, or on Ground,
And but one sorry Bed was to be found:
And that so little it would hold but one,
Though till this Hour they never lay alone.

    So were they forc'd to part; one stay'd behind,
His Fellow sought what Lodging he could find:
At last he found a Stall where Oxen stood,
And that he rather chose than lie abroad.
'Twas in a farther Yard without a Door,
But for his ease, well litter'd was the Floor.

    His Fellow, who the narrow Bed had kept,
Was weary, and without a Rocker slept:
Supine he snor'd; but in the dead of Night,
He dreamt his Friend appear'd before his Sight,
Who with a ghastly Look and doleful Cry,
Said help me Brother, or this Night I die:
Arise, and help, before all Help be vain,
Or in an Oxes Stall I shall be slain.

    Rowz'd from his Rest he waken'd in a start,
Shiv'ring with Horror, and with aking Heart;
At length to cure himself by Reason tries;
'Twas but a Dream, and what are Dreams but Lies?
So thinking chang'd his Side, and clos'd his Eyes.
His Dream returns; his Friend appears again,
The Murd'rers come; now help, or I am slain:
'Twas but a Vision still, and Visions are but vain.

    He dreamt the third: But now his Friend appear'd
Pale, naked, pierc'd with Wounds, with Blood besmear'd:
Thrice warn'd awake, said he; Relief is late,

The Deed is done; but thou revenge my Fate:
Tardy of Aid, unseal thy heavy Eyes,
Awake, and with the dawning Day arise:
Take to the Western Gate thy ready way,
For by that Passage they my Corps convey:
My Corpse is in a Tumbril laid; among
The Filth, and Ordure, and enclos'd with Dung.
That Cart arrest, and raise a common Cry,
For sacred hunger of my Gold I die;
Then shew'd his grisly Wounds; and last he drew
A piteous Sigh; and took a long Adieu.

    The frighted Friend arose by break of Day,
And found the Stall where late his Fellow lay.
Then of his impious Host enquiring more,
Was answer'd that his Guest was gone before:
Muttring he went, said he, by Morning-light,
And much complain'd of his ill Rest by Night.
This rais'd Suspicion in the Pilgrim's Mind;
Because all Hosts are of an evil Kind,
And oft, to share the Spoil, with Robbers join'd.

    His Dream confirm'd his Thought: with troubled
        Look
Strait to the Western-Gate his way he took.
There, as his Dream foretold, a Cart he found,
That carry'd Composs forth to dung the Ground.
This, when the Pilgrim saw, he stretch'd his Throat,
And cry'd out Murther, with a yelling Note.
My murther'd Fellow in this Cart lies dead,
Vengeance and Justice on the Villain's Head.
You, Magistrates, who sacred Laws dispense,
On you I call to punish this Offence.

    The Word thus giv'n, within a little space,

The Mob came roaring out, and throng'd the Place.
All in a trice they cast the Cart to Ground,
And in the Dung the murther'd Body found;
Though breathless, warm, and reeking from the Wound.
Good Heav'n, whose darling Attribute we find
Is boundless Grace, and Mercy to Mankind,
Abhors the Cruel; and the Deeds of Night
By wond'rous Ways reveals in open Light:
Murther may pass unpunished for a time,
But tardy Justice will o'ertake the Crime.
And oft a speedier Pain the Guilty feels;
The Hue and Cry of Heav'n pursues him at the Heels,
Fresh from the Fact; as in the present Case;
The Criminals are seiz'd upon the Place:
Carter and Host confronted Face to Face.
Stiff in denial, as the Law appoints
On Engins they distend their tortur'd Joints:
So was Confession forc'd, th' Offence was known,
And publick Justice on th' Offenders done.

    Here may you see that Visions are to dread:
And in the Page that follows this; I read
Of two young Merchants, whom the hope of Gain
Induc'd in Partnership to cross the Main:
Waiting till willing Winds their Sails supply'd,
Within a Trading-Town they long abide,
Full fairly situate on a Haven's side.

    One Evening it befel that looking out,
The Wind they long had wish'd was come about:
Well pleas'd they went to Rest; and if the Gale
'Till Morn continu'd, both resolv'd to sail.
But as together in a Bed they lay,

The younger had a Dream at break of Day.
A Man, he thought, stood frowning at his side;
Who warn'd him for his Safety to provide,
Not put to Sea, but safe on Shore abide.
I come, thy Genius, to command thy stay;
Trust not the Winds, for fatal is the Day,
And Death unhop'd attends the watry way.
  The Vision said: And vanish'd from his sight,
The Dreamer waken'd in a mortal Fright:
Then pull'd his drowzy Neighbour, and declar'd
What in his Slumber he had seen, and heard.
His Friend smil'd scornful, and with proud contempt
Rejects as idle what his Fellow dreamt.
Stay, who will stay: For me no Fears restrain,
Who follow *Mercury* the God of Gain:
Let each Man do as to his Fancy seems,
I wait, not I, till you have better Dreams.
Dreams are but Interludes, which Fancy makes,
When Monarch-Reason sleeps, this Mimick wakes:
Compounds a Medley of disjointed Things,
A Mob of Coblers, and a Court of Kings:
Light Fumes are merry, grosser Fumes are sad;
Both are the reasonable Soul run mad:
And many monstrous Forms in sleep we see,
That neither were, nor are, nor e'er can be.
Sometimes, forgotten Things long cast behind
Rush forward in the Brain, and come to mind.
The Nurses Legends are for Truths receiv'd,
And the Man dreams but what the Boy believ'd.
  Sometimes we but rehearse a former Play,
The Night restores our Actions done by Day;

As Hounds in sleep will open for their Prey.
In short, the Farce of Dreams is of a piece,
Chimera's all; and more absurd, or less:
You, who believe in Tales, abide alone,
What e'er I get this Voyage is my own.

  Thus while he spoke he heard the shouting Crew
That call'd aboard, and took his last adieu.
The Vessel went before a merry Gale,
And for quick Passage put on ev'ry Sail:
But when least fear'd, and ev'n in open Day,
The Mischief overtook her in the way:
Whether she sprung a Leak, I cannot find,
Or whether she was overset with Wind;
Or that some Rock below, her bottom rent,
But down at once with all her Crew she went;
Her Fellow Ships from far her Loss descry'd;
But only she was sunk, and all were safe beside.

  By this Example you are taught again,
That Dreams and Visions are not always vain:
But if, dear Partlet, you are yet in doubt,
Another Tale shall make the former out.

  Kenelm the Son of *Kenulph*, *Mercia*'s King,
Whose holy Life the Legends loudly sing,
Warn'd, in a Dream, his Murther did foretel
From Point to Point as after it befel:
All Circumstances to his Nurse he told,
(A Wonder, from a Child of sev'n Years old:)
The Dream with Horror heard, the good old Wife
From Treason counsell'd him to guard his Life:
But close to keep the Secret in his Mind,
For a Boy's Vision small Belief would find.

The pious Child, by Promise bound, obey'd,
Nor was the fatal Murther long delay'd:
By *Quenda* slain he fell before his time,
Made a young Martyr by his Sister's Crime.
The Tale is told by venerable *Bede*,
Which, at your better leisure, you may read.
     Macrobius too relates the Vision sent
To the great *Scipio* with the fam'd event,
Objections makes, but after makes Replies,
And adds, that Dreams are often Prophecies.
     Of *Daniel*, you may read in Holy Writ,
Who, when the King his Vision did forget,
Cou'd Word for Word the wond'rous Dream repeat.
Nor less of Patriarch *Joseph* understand
Who by a Dream inslav'd th' *Egyptian* Land,
The Years of Plenty and of Dearth foretold,
When for their Bread, their Liberty they sold.
Nor must th' exalted Buttler be forgot,
Nor he whose Dream presag'd his hanging Lot.
     And did not *Crœsus* the same Death foresee,
Rais'd in his Vision on a lofty Tree?
The Wife of *Hector* in his utmost Pride,
Dreamt of his Death the Night before he dy'd:
Well was he warn'd from Battle to refrain,
But Men to Death decreed are warn'd in vain:
He dar'd the Dream, and by his fatal Foe was slain.
     Much more I know, which I forbear to speak,
For see the ruddy Day begins to break:
Let this suffice, that plainly I foresee
My Dream was bad, and bodes Adversity:
But neither Pills nor Laxatives I like,

They only serve to make a well-man sick:
Of these his Gain the sharp Phisician makes,
And often gives a Purge, but seldom takes:
They not correct, but poyson all the Blood,
And ne'er did any but the Doctors good.
Their Tribe, Trade, Trinkets, I defy them all,
With ev'ry Work of 'Pothecary's Hall.
   These melancholy Matters I forbear:
But let me tell Thee, Partlet mine, and swear,
That when I view the Beauties of thy Face,
I fear not Death, nor Dangers, nor Disgrace:
So may my Soul have Bliss, as when I spy
The Scarlet Red about thy Partridge Eye,
While thou art constant to thy own true Knight,
While thou art mine, and I am thy delight,
All Sorrows at thy Presence take their flight.
For true it is, as *in Principio*,
Mulier est hominis confusio.
Madam, the meaning of this Latin is,
That Woman is to Man his Soveraign Bliss.
For when by Night I feel your tender Side,
Though for the narrow Perch I cannot ride,
Yet I have such a Solace in my Mind,
That all my boding Cares are cast behind:
And ev'n already I forget my Dream;
He said, and downward flew from off the Beam.
For Day-light now began apace to spring,
The Thrush to whistle, and the Lark to sing.
Then crowing clap'd his Wings, th' appointed call
To chuck his Wives together in the Hall.
   By this the Widow had unbarr'd the Door,

And Chanticleer went strutting out before,
With Royal Courage, and with Heart so light,
As shew'd he scorn'd the Visions of the Night.
Now roaming in the Yard he spurn'd the Ground,
And gave to Partlet the first Grain he found.
Then often feather'd her with wanton Play,
And trod her twenty times e'er prime of Day;
And took by turns and gave so much delight,
Her Sisters pin'd with Envy at the sight.

     He chuck'd again, when other Corns he found,
And scarcely deign'd to set a Foot to Ground.
But swagger'd like a Lord about his Hall,
And his sev'n Wives came running at his call.

     'Twas now the Month in which the World began,
(If *March* beheld the first created Man:)
And since the vernal Equinox, the Sun,
In *Aries* twelve Degrees, or more had run,
When casting up his Eyes against the Light,
Both Month, and Day, and Hour he measur'd right;
And told more truly, than th' Ephemeris,
For Art may err, but Nature cannot miss.

     Thus numb'ring Times, and Seasons in his Breast,
His second crowing the third Hour confess'd.
Then turning, said to Partlet, See, my Dear,
How lavish Nature has adorn'd the Year;
How the pale Primrose, and blue Violet spring,
And Birds essay their Throats disus'd to sing:
All these are ours; and I with pleasure see
Man strutting on two Legs, and aping me!
An unfledg'd Creature, of a lumpish frame,
Indew'd with fewer Particles of Flame:

Our Dame sits couring o'er a Kitchin-fire,
I draw fresh Air, and Nature's Works admire:
And ev'n this Day, in more delight abound,
Than since I was an Egg, I ever found.

      The time shall come when Chanticleer shall wish
His Words unsaid, and hate his boasted Bliss:
The crested Bird shall by Experience know,
Jove made not him his Master-piece below;
And learn the latter end of Joy is Woe.
The Vessel of his Bliss to Dregs is run,
And Heav'n will have him tast his other Tun.

      Ye Wise draw near, and hearken to my Tale,
Which proves that oft the Proud by Flatt'ry fall:
The Legend is as true I undertake
As *Tristram* is, and *Launcelot* of the Lake:
Which all our Ladies in such rev'rence hold,
As if in Book of Martyrs it were told.

      A Fox full fraught with seeming Sanctity,
That fear'd an Oath, but like the Devil, would lie,
Who look'd like Lent, and had the holy Leer,
And durst not sin before he say'd his Pray'r:
This pious Cheat that never suck'd the Blood,
Nor chaw'd the Flesh of Lambs but when he cou'd,
Had pass'd three Summers in the neighb'ring Wood;
And musing long, whom next to circumvent,
On Chanticleer his wicked Fancy bent:
And in his high Imagination cast,
By Stratagem to gratify his Tast.

      The Plot contriv'd, before the break of Day,
Saint *Reynard* through the Hedge had made his way;
The Pale was next, but proudly with a bound
He lept the Fence of the forbidden Ground:

Yet fearing to be seen, within a Bed
Of Colworts he conceal'd his wily Head;
There sculk'd till Afternoon, and watch'd his time,
(As Murd'rers use) to perpetrate his Crime.

      O Hypocrite, ingenious to destroy,
O Traytor, worse than *Sinon* was to *Troy*;
O vile Subverter of the *Gallick* Reign,
More false than *Gano* was to *Charlemaign*!
O Chanticleer, in an unhappy Hour
Did'st thou forsake the Safety of thy Bow'r:
Better for Thee thou had'st believ'd thy Dream,
And not that Day descended from the Beam!

      But here the Doctors eagerly dispute:
Some hold Predestination absolute:
Some Clerks maintain, that Heav'n at first foresees,
And in the virtue of Foresight decrees.
If this be so, then Prescience binds the Will,
And Mortals are not free to Good or Ill:
For what he first foresaw, he must ordain,
Or its eternal Prescience may be vain:
As bad for us as Prescience had not bin:
For first, or last, he's Author of the Sin.
And who says that, let the blaspheming Man
Say worse ev'n of the Devil, if he can.
For how can that Eternal Pow'r be just
To punish Man, who Sins because he must?
Or, how can He reward a vertuous Deed,
Which is not done by us; but first decreed?

      I cannot boult this Matter to the Bran,
As *Bradwardin* and holy *Austin* can:
If Prescience can determine Actions so
That we must do, because he did foreknow;

Or that foreknowing, yet our choice is free,
Not forc'd to Sin by strict necessity:
This strict necessity they simple call,
Another sort there is conditional.
The first so binds the Will, that Things foreknown
By Spontaneity, not Choice, are done.
Thus Galley-Slaves tug willing, at their Oar,
Consent to work, in prospect of the Shore;
But wou'd not work at all, if not constrain'd before.
That other does not Liberty constrain,
But Man may either act, or may refrain.
Heav'n made us Agents free to Good or Ill,
And forc'd it not, tho' he foresaw the Will.
Freedom was first bestow'd on human Race,
And Prescience only held the second place.
      If he could make such Agents wholly free,
I not dispute; the Point's too high for me;
For Heav'n's unfathom'd Pow'r what Man can sound,
Or put to his Omnipotence a Bound?
He made us to his Image all agree;
That Image is the Soul, and that must be,
Or not the Maker's Image, or be free.
      But whether it were better Man had been
By Nature bound to Good, not free to Sin,
I wave, for fear of splitting on a Rock,
The Tale I tell is only of a Cock;
Who had not run the hazard of his Life
Had he believ'd his Dream, and not his Wife:
For Women, with a mischief to their Kind,
Pervert, with bad Advice, our better Mind.
A Woman's Counsel brought us first to Woe,

And made her Man his Paradice forego,
Where at Heart's ease he liv'd; and might have bin
As free from Sorrow as he was from Sin.
For what the Devil had their Sex to do,
That, born to Folly, they presum'd to know,
And could not see the Serpent in the Grass?
But I my self presume, and let it pass.

     Silence in times of Suff'ring is the best,
'Tis dang'rous to disturb a Hornet's Nest.
In other Authors you may find enough,
But all they say of Dames is idle Stuff.
Legends of lying Wits together bound,
The Wife of *Bath* would throw 'em to the Ground:
These are the Words of Chanticleer, not mine,
I honor Dames, and think their Sex divine.

     Now to continue what my Tale begun.
Lay Madam Partlet basking in the Sun,
Breast-high in Sand: Her Sisters in a row,
Enjoy'd the Beams above, the Warmth below.
The Cock that of his Flesh was ever free,
Sung merrier than the Mermaid in the Sea:
And so befel, that as he cast his Eye,
Among the Colworts on a Butterfly,
He saw false *Reynard* where he lay full low,
I need not swear he had no list to Crow:
But cry'd Cock, Cock, and gave a suddain start,
As sore dismaid and frighted at his Heart.
For Birds and Beasts, inform'd by Nature, know
Kinds opposite to theirs, and fly their Foe.
So, Chanticleer, who never saw a Fox,
Yet shun'd him as a Sailor shuns the Rocks.

But the false Loon who cou'd not work his Will
By open Force, employ'd his flatt'ring Skill;
I hope, my Lord, said he, I not offend,
Are you afraid of me, that am your Friend?
I were a Beast indeed to do you wrong,
I, who have lov'd and honour'd you so long:
Stay, gentle Sir, nor take a false Alarm,
For on my Soul I never meant you harm.
I come no Spy, nor as a Traytor press,
To learn the Secrets of your soft Recess:
Far be from *Reynard* so prophane a Thought,
But by the sweetness of your Voice was brought:
For, as I bid my Beads, by chance I heard,
The Song as of an Angel in the Yard:
A Song that wou'd have charm'd th' infernal Gods,
And banish'd Horror from the dark Abodes:
Had *Orpheus* sung it in the neather Sphere,
So much the Hymn had pleas'd the Tyrant's Ear,
The Wife had been detain'd, to keep the Husband there.
    My Lord, your Sire familiarly I knew,
A Peer deserving such a Son, as you:
He, with your Lady-Mother (whom Heav'n rest)
Has often grac'd my House, and been my Guest:
To view his living Features does me good,
For I am your poor Neighbour in the Wood;
And in my Cottage shou'd be proud to see
The worthy Heir of my Friend's Family.
    But since I speak of Singing let me say,
As with an upright Heart I safely may,
That, save your self, there breaths not on the Ground,
One like your Father for a Silver sound.

So sweetly wou'd he wake the Winter-day,
That Matrons to the Church mistook their way,
And thought they heard the merry Organ play.
And he to raise his Voice with artful Care,
(What will not Beaux attempt to please the Fair?)
On Tiptoe stood to sing with greater Strength,
And stretch'd his comely Neck at all the length:
And while he pain'd his Voice to pierce the Skies,
As Saints in Raptures use, would shut his Eyes,
That the sound striving through the narrow Throat,
His winking might avail, to mend the Note.
By this, in Song, he never had his Peer,
From sweet *Cecilia* down to Chanticleer;
Not *Maro*'s Muse who sung the mighty Man,
Nor *Pindar*'s heav'nly Lyre, nor *Horace* when a Swan.
Your Ancestors proceed from Race divine,
From *Brennus* and *Belinus* is your Line:
Who gave to sov'raign *Rome* such loud Alarms,
That ev'n the Priests were not excus'd from Arms.
     Besides, a famous Monk of modern times,
Has left of Cocks recorded in his Rhimes,
That of a Parish-Priest the Son and Heir,
(When Sons of Priests were from the Proverb clear)
Affronted once a Cock of noble Kind,
And either lam'd his Legs, or struck him blind;
For which the Clerk his Father was disgrac'd,
And in his Benefice another plac'd.
Now sing, my Lord, if not for love of me,
Yet for the sake of sweet Saint Charity;
Make Hills, and Dales, and Earth and Heav'n rejoice,
And emulate your Father's Angel-voice.

The Cock was pleas'd to hear him speak so fair,
And proud beside, as solar People are:
Nor cou'd the Treason from the Truth descry,
So was he ravish'd with this Flattery:
So much the more as from a little Elf,
He had a high Opinion of himself:
Though sickly, slender, and not large of Limb,
Concluding all the World was made for him.

     Ye Princes rais'd by Poets to the Gods,
And *Alexander'd* up in lying Odes,
Believe not ev'ry flatt'ring Knave's report,
There's many a *Reynard* lurking in the Court;
And he shall be receiv'd with more regard
And list'ned to, than modest Truth is heard.

     This Chanticleer of whom the Story sings,
Stood high upon his Toes, and clap'd his Wings;
Then stretch'd his Neck, and wink'd with both his Eyes;
Ambitious, as he sought, th' Olympick Prize.
But while he pain'd himself to raise his Note,
False *Reynard* rush'd, and caught him by the Throat.
Then on his Back he laid the precious Load,
And sought his wonted shelter of the Wood;
Swiftly he made his way, the Mischief done,
Of all unheeded, and pursu'd by none.

     Alas, what stay is there in human State,
Or who can shun inevitable Fate?
The Doom was written, the Decree was past,
E'er the Foundations of the World were cast!
In *Aries* though the Sun exalted stood,
His Patron-Planet to procure his good;
Yet *Saturn* was his mortal Foe, and he

In *Libra* rais'd, oppos'd the same Degree:
The Rays both good and bad, of equal Pow'r,
Each thwarting other made a mingled Hour.

On *Friday*-morn he dreamt this direful Dream,
Cross to the worthy Native, in his Scheme!
Ah blissful *Venus*, Goddess of Delight,
How cou'd'st thou suffer thy devoted Knight,
On thy own Day to fall by Foe oppress'd,
The wight of all the World who serv'd thee best?
Who true to Love, was all for Recreation,
And minded not the Work of Propagation.
Gaufride, who could'st so well in Rhime complain,
The Death of *Richard* with an Arrow slain,
Why had not I thy Muse, or thou my Heart,
To sing this heavy Dirge with equal Art!
That I like thee on *Friday* might complain;
For on that Day was *Ceur de Lion* slain.

Not louder Cries when *Ilium* was in Flames,
Were sent to Heav'n by woful *Trojan* Dames,
When *Pyrrhus* toss'd on high his burnish'd Blade,
And offer'd *Priam* to his Father's Shade,
Than for the Cock the widow'd Poultry made.
Fair Partlet first, when he was born from sight,
With soveraign Shrieks bewail'd her Captive Knight.
Far lowder than the *Carthaginian* Wife,
When *Asdrubal* her Husband lost his Life,
When she beheld the smouldring Flames ascend,
And all the *Punick* Glories at an end:
Willing into the Fires she plung'd her Head,
With greater Ease than others seek their Bed.
Not more aghast the Matrons of Renown,

When Tyrant *Nero* burn'd th' Imperial Town,
Shriek'd for the downfal in a doleful Cry,
For which their guiltless Lords were doom'd to die.
    Now to my Story I return again.
The trembling Widow, and her Daughters twain,
This woful cackling Cry with Horror heard,
Of those distracted Damsels in the Yard;
And starting up beheld the heavy Sight,
How *Reynard* to the Forest took his Flight,
And cross his Back as in triumphant Scorn,
The Hope and Pillar of the House was born.
    The Fox, the wicked Fox, was all the Cry,
Out from his House ran ev'ry Neighbour nigh:
The Vicar first, and after him the Crew,
With Forks and Staves the Fellon to pursue.
Ran *Coll* our Dog, and *Talbot* with the Band,
And *Malkin*, with her Distaff in her Hand:
Ran Cow and Calf, and Family of Hogs,
In Panique Horror of pursuing Dogs,
With many a deadly Grunt and doleful Squeak
Poor Swine, as if their pretty Hearts would break.
The Shouts of Men, the Women in dismay,
With Shrieks augment the Terror of the Day.
The Ducks that heard the Proclamation cry'd,
And fear'd a Persecution might betide,
Full twenty Mile from Town their Voyage take,
Obscure in Rushes of the liquid Lake.
The Geese fly o'er the Barn; the Bees in Arms,
Drive headlong from their Waxen Cells in Swarms.
Jack Straw at *London*-stone with all his Rout
Struck not the City with so loud a Shout;

Not when with *English* Hate they did pursue
A *French* Man, or an unbelieving *Jew*:
Not when the Welkin rung with one and all;
And Echoes bounded back from *Fox*'s Hall;
Earth seem'd to sink beneath, and Heav'n above to fall.
With Might and Main they chas'd the murd'rous Fox,
With brazen Trumpets, and inflated Box,
To kindle *Mars* with military Sounds,
Nor wanted Horns t' inspire sagacious Hounds.

    But see how Fortune can confound the Wise,
And when they least expect it, turn the Dice.
The Captive Cock, who scarce cou'd draw his Breath,
And lay within the very Jaws of Death;
Yet in this Agony his Fancy wrought
And Fear supply'd him with this happy Thought:
Yours is the Prize, victorious Prince, said he,
The Vicar my defeat, and all the Village see.
Enjoy your friendly Fortune while you may,
And bid the Churls that envy you the Prey,
Call back their mungril Curs, and cease their Cry,
See Fools, the shelter of the Wood is nigh,
And Chanticleer in your despight shall die.
He shall be pluck'd, and eaten to the Bone.

    'Tis well advis'd, in Faith it shall be done;
This *Reynard* said: but as the Word he spoke,
The Pris'ner with a Spring from Prison broke:
Then stretch'd his feather'd Fans with all his might,
And to the neighb'ring Maple wing'd his flight.

    Whom when the Traytor safe on Tree beheld,
He curs'd the Gods, with Shame and Sorrow fill'd;
Shame for his Folly; Sorrow out of time,

For Plotting an unprofitable Crime:
Yet mast'ring both, th' Artificer of Lies
Renews th' Assault, and his last Batt'ry tries.

      Though I, said he, did ne'er in Thought offend,
How justly may my Lord suspect his Friend?
Th' appearance is against me, I confess,
Who seemingly have put you in Distress:
You, if your Goodness does not plead my Cause,
May think I broke all hospitable Laws,
To bear you from your Palace-yard by Might,
And put your noble Person in a Fright:
This, since you take it ill, I must repent,
Though Heav'n can witness with no bad intent,
I practis'd it, to make you taste your Cheer,
With double Pleasure first prepar'd by fear.
So loyal Subjects often seize their Prince,
Forc'd (for his Good) to seeming Violence,
Yet mean his sacred Person not the least Offence.
Descend; so help me *Jove* as you shall find
That *Reynard* comes of no dissembling Kind.

      Nay, quoth the Cock; but I beshrew us both,
If I believe a Saint upon his Oath:
An honest Man may take a Knave's Advice,
But Idiots only will be couzen'd twice:
Once warn'd is well bewar'd: No flatt'ring Lies
Shall sooth me more to sing with winking Eyes,
And open Mouth, for fear of catching Flies.
Who Blindfold walks upon a Rivers brim
When he should see, has he deserv'd to swim?
Better, Sir Cock, let all Contention cease,
Come down, said *Reynard*, let us treat of Peace.

A Peace with all my Soul, said Chanticleer;
But with your Favour, I will treat it here:
And least the Truce with Treason should be mixt,
'Tis my concern to have the Tree betwixt.

The MORAL: *In this plain Fable you th' Effect may see*
Of Negligence, and fond Credulity:
And learn besides of Flatt'rers to beware,
Then most pernicious when they speak too fair.
The Cock and Fox, the Fool and Knave imply;
The Truth is moral, though the Tale a Lie.
Who spoke in Parables, I dare not say;
But sure, he knew it was a pleasing way,
Sound Sense, by plain Example, to convey.
And in a Heathen Author we may find
That Pleasure with Instruction should be join'd:
So take the Corn, and leave the Chaff behind.

—JOHN DRYDEN

The Fable of the Belly and the Members

D R A M A

MENENIUS AGRIPPA.   . . . I shall tell you
  A pretty tale. It may be you have heard it;
  But, since it serves my purpose, I will venture
  To stale't a little more.

1ST CITIZEN.   Well, I'll hear it, sir. Yet you must not
  think to fob off our disgrace with a tale. But, an't please
  you, deliver.

MEN.   There was a time when all the body's members
  Rebell'd against the belly, thus accus'd it:
  That only like a gulf it did remain
  I' th' midst o' th' body, idle and unactive,
  Still cupboarding the viand, never bearing
  Like labour with the rest; where th' other instruments
  Did see and hear, devise, instruct, walk, feel,
  And, mutually participate, did minister
  Unto the appetite and affection common
  Of the whole body. The belly answer'd—

CIT.   Well, sir, what answer made the belly?

MEN.   Sir, I shall tell you. With a kind of smile,
  Which ne'er came from the lungs, but even thus—
  For look you, I may make the belly smile
  As well as speak—it tauntingly replied

218:

To the discontented members, the mutinous parts
That envied his receipt; even so most fitly
As you malign our senators for that
They are not such as you.

CIT.   Your belly's answer—What?
The kingly crowned head, the vigilant eye,
The counsellor heart, the arm our soldier,
Our steed the leg, the tongue our trumpeter,
With other muniments and petty helps
In this our fabric, if that they—

MEN.   What then?
Fore me, this fellow speaks! What then? What then?

CIT.   Should by the cormorant belly be restrain'd,
Who is the sink o' th' body—

MEN.   Well, what then?

CIT.   The former agents, if they did complain,
What could the belly answer?

MEN.   I will tell you.
If you'll bestow a small—of what you have little—
Patience awhile, you'st hear the belly's answer.

CIT.   Y're long about it.

MEN.   Note me this, good friend:
Your most grave belly was deliberate,
Not rash like his accusers, and thus answered:
'True is it, my incorporate friends,' quoth he,

'That I receive the general food at first,
Which you do live upon; and fit it is,
Because I am the storehouse and the shop
Of the whole body. But, if you do remember,
I send it through the rivers of your blood,
Even to the court, the heart, to th' seat o' th' brain;
And, through the cranks and offices of man,
The strongest nerves and small inferior veins
From me receive that natural competency
Whereby they live. And though that all at once
You, my good friends'—this says the belly; mark me.

CIT.　Aye, sir; well, well.

MEN.　　　　　　　'Though all at once cannot
　　See what I do deliver out to each,
　　Yet I can make my audit up, that all
　　From me do back receive the flour of all,
　　And leave me but the bran.' What say you to't?

CIT.　It was an answer. How apply you this?

MEN.　The senators of Rome are this good belly,
　　And you the mutinous members; for, examine
　　Their counsels and their cares, digest things rightly
　　Touching the weal o' th' common, you shall find
　　No public benefit which you receive
　　But it proceeds or comes from them to you
　　And no way from yourselves. . . .

—WILLIAM SHAKESPEARE
(from *Coriolanus*, Act I, Scene 1)

The Lady and the Bear

N U R S E R Y   R H Y M E

A Lady came to a Bear by a Stream.
    "O why are you fishing that way?
Tell me, dear Bear there by the Stream,
Why are you fishing that way?"

"I am what is known as a Biddly Bear,—
That's why I'm fishing this way.
We Biddly's are Pee-culiar Bears.
And so,—I'm fishing this way.

"And besides, it seems there's a Law:
A most, most exactious Law
Says a Bear
Doesn't dare
Doesn't dare
Doesn't DARE
Use a Hook or a Line,
Or an old piece of Twine,
Not even the end of his Claw, Claw, Claw,
Not even the end of his Claw.
Yes, a Bear has to fish with his Paw, Paw, Paw.
A Bear has to fish with his Paw."

"O it's Wonderful how with a flick of your Wrist,
You can fish out a fish, out a fish, out a fish,
If *I* were a fish I just couldn't resist

You, when you are fishing that way, that way,
When you are fishing that way."

And at that the Lady slipped from the Bank
And fell in the Stream still clutching a Plank,
But the Bear just sat there until
                she Sank;
As he went on fishing his way, his way,
As he went on fishing his way.

—THEODORE ROETHKE

The Plot Against the Giant

POEM

First Girl

When this yokel comes maundering,
  Whetting his hacker,
I shall run before him,
Diffusing the civilest odors
Out of geraniums and unsmelled flowers.
It will check him.

Second Girl

I shall run before him,
Arching cloths besprinkled with colors
As small as fish-eggs.
The threads
Will abash him.

Third Girl

Oh, la . . . le pauvre!
I shall run before him,
With a curious puffing.
He will bend his ear then.
I shall whisper
Heavenly labials in a world of gutturals.
It will undo him.

—WALLACE STEVENS

On Angels

The death of God left the angels in a strange position. They were overtaken suddenly by a fundamental question. One can attempt to imagine the moment. How did they *look* at the instant the question invaded them, flooding the angelic consciousness, taking hold with terrifying force? The question was, "What are angels?"

New to questioning, unaccustomed to terror, unskilled in aloneness, the angels (we assume) fell into despair.

The question of what angels "are" has a considerable history. Swedenborg, for example, talked to a great many angels and faithfully recorded what they told him. Angels look like human beings, Swedenborg says. "That angels are human forms, or men, has been seen by me a thousand times." And again: "From all of my experience, which is now of many years, I am able to state that angels are wholly men in form, having faces, eyes, ears, bodies, arms, hands, and feet . . ." But a man cannot see angels with his bodily eyes, only with the eyes of the spirit.

Swedenborg has a great deal more to say about angels, all of the highest interest: that no angel is ever permitted to stand behind another and look at the back of his head, for this would disturb the influx of good and truth from the Lord; that angels have the east, where the Lord is seen as a sun, always before their eyes; and that angels are clothed according to their intelligence. "Some of the most intelligent have garments that blaze as if with flame, others have garments that glisten as if with light; the less intelligent have garments that are glistening white or white without the effulgence; and the still less intelligent have garments of various colors. But the angels of the inmost heaven are not clothed."

All of this (presumably) no longer obtains.

Gustav Davidson, in his useful *Dictionary of Angels*, has brought together much of what is known about them. Their names are called: the angel Elubatel, the angel Friagne, the angel Gaap, the angel Hatiphas (genius of finery), the angel Murmur (a fallen angel), the angel Mqttro, the angel Or, the angel Rash, the angel Sandalphon (taller than a five hundred years' journey on foot), the angel Smat. Davidson distinguishes categories: Angels of Quaking, who surround the heavenly throne; Masters of Howling and Lords of Shouting, whose work is praise; messengers, mediators, watchers, warners. Davidson's *Dictionary* is a very large book; his bibliography lists more than eleven hundred items.

The former angelic consciousness has been most beautifully described by Joseph Lyons (in a paper titled *The Psychology of Angels*, published in 1957). Each angel, Lyons says, knows all that there is to know about himself and every other angel. "No angel could ever ask a question, because questioning proceeds out of a situation of not knowing, and of being in some way aware of not knowing. An angel cannot be curious; he has nothing to be curious about. He cannot wonder. Knowing all that there is to know, the world of possible knowledge must appear to him as an ordered set of facts which is completely behind him, completely fixed and certain and within his grasp . . ."

But this, too, no longer obtains.

It is a curiosity of writing about angels that, very often, one turns out to be writing about men. The themes are twinned. Thus one finally learns that Lyons, for example, is really writing not about angels but about schizophrenics—thinking about men by invoking angels. And this holds true of much other writing on the subject—a point, we may assume, that was not lost on the angels when they began considering their new relation to the cosmos, when the analogues (is an angel more like a quetzal or more like a man? or more like music?) were being handed about.

We may further assume that some attempt was made at self-definition by function. An angel is what he does. Thus it was necessary to investigate possible new roles (you are reminded that this is impure speculation). After the lamentation had gone on for hundreds and hundreds of whatever the angels use for time, an angel proposed that lamentation be the function of angels eternally, as adoration was formerly. The mode of lamentation would be silence, in contrast to the unceasing chanting of Glorias that had been their former employment. But it is not in the nature of angels to be silent.

A counter-proposal was that the angels affirm chaos. There were to be five great proofs of the existence of chaos, of which the first was the absence of God. The other four could surely be located. The work of definition and explication could, if done nicely enough, occupy the angels forever, as the contrary work has occupied human theologians. But there is not much enthusiasm for chaos among the angels.

The most serious because most radical proposal considered by the angels was refusal—that they would re-move themselves from being, not be. The tremendous dignity that would accrue to the angels by this act was felt to be a manifestation of spiritual pride. Refusal was refused.

There were other suggestions, more subtle and com-plicated, less so, none overwhelmingly attractive.

I saw a famous angel on television; his garments glistened as if with light. He talked about the situation of angels now. Angels, he said, are like men *in some ways*. The problem of adoration is felt to be central. He said that for a time the angels had tried adoring each other, as we do, but had found it, finally, "not enough." He said they are continuing to search for a new principle.

—DONALD BARTHELME

Part Two

"Fables are a succession
of changes."

—G. E. Lessing

The Fox and Deer

As Fox was going along he met a Deer with two spotted fawns beside her. "What have you done," said he, "to make your children spotted like that?" "I made a big fire of cedar wood and placed them before it. The sparks thrown off burned the spots which you see," answered the Deer. Fox was pleased with the color of the fawns, so he went home and told his children to gather cedar wood for a large fire. When the fire was burning well, he put the young foxes in a row before the fire, as he supposed the Deer had done. When he noticed that they did not change color, he pushed them into the fire and covered them with ashes, thinking he had not applied sufficient heat at first. As the fire went out, he saw their white teeth gleaming where the heat had curled back the skin into a smile. "Ah, you will be very pretty now." Fox pulled his offspring from the ashes, expecting to find them much changed in color, and so they were—black, shriveled, and dead.

—AMERICAN INDIAN
composite by Karen Kennerly

Mother Crab

Mother to little crab:
"Learn not to sidle!
Don't go rambling rockpools on the bias!"
"Mother, Mistress of Studies, you first
    march straight forward—
and when I see you do it, so can I."

—BABRIUS

translated by Robert Fitzgerald

The Carthorses and the Saddlehorse*

Two carthorses, a gelding and a mare, were brought to Samoa, and put in the same field with a saddlehorse to run free on the island. They were rather afraid to go near him, for they saw he was a saddlehorse, and supposed he would not speak to them. Now the saddlehorse had never seen creatures so big. "These must be great chiefs," thought he, and he approached them civilly. "Lady and gentleman," said he, "I understand you are from the colonies. I offer you my affectionate compliments, and make you heartily welcome to the island."

The colonials looked at him askance, and consulted with each other.

"Who can he be?" said the gelding.

"He seems suspiciously civil," said the mare.

"I do not think he can be much account," said the gelding.

"Depend upon it he is only a Kanaka," said the mare.

Then they turned to him.

"Go to the devil!" said the gelding.

"I wonder at your impudence, speaking to persons of our quality!" cried the mare.

The saddlehorse went away by himself. "I was right," said he, "they are great chiefs."

—ROBERT LOUIS STEVENSON

* This fable is also found in the Gaelic folk literature of West Kerry, Ireland.

The Feather-Eared Owl and the Blind Ass

A blind ass wandered off-course in a forest. (He had set out on a very long journey.) By dusk this foolish beast, so entangled in brambles, couldn't move at all—forward or backward. (Granted, even a sharp-eyed ass would have had trouble.)

Luckily an owl was watching close by, and took it upon himself to play guide to the ass. (Feather-eared owls, it's well known, are keen-sighted at night.) Precipices, ditches, hillocks, and mounds—all these the owl spotted as if it were noon. By morning, together, they had struck a clear path.

How could one do without such a guide? The ass asked the owl to keep company with him; for he had gotten the idea of crisscrossing the world. The owl perched imperiously on the ass's long neck. They took to the road. And was this journeying happy?

No.

Hardly had dawn begun to light up the sky, when, to the owl's eyes, all went blacker than night. However our lordship the owl was obstinate. His counsel by turn swerved them off the road, and back on. "Watch it," he warned, "there's a puddle to the right." But there was no puddle, and to the left it was worse. "Still further left, left one more step!"

With a crash the ass and the feather-eared owl dropped down a ravine.

—IVAN KRYLOV

translated by Martin Lopez-Morillas and Karen Kennerly

Treachery

Oysters open completely when the moon is full; and when the crab sees one it throws a piece of stone or seaweed into it and the oyster cannot close again so that it serves the crab for its meat.

So it is with him who opens his mouth to tell a secret and thereby puts himself at the mercy of the listener.

—LEONARDO DA VINCI

The Rat and the Oyster

A rat, a field rat, a feeble-minded rat,
one day decided he was weary of home—
abandoned thereupon his fields and sheaves,
wandered the countryside, leaving his hole
behind. No sooner were familiar surroundings
out of sight, than the world, he said, was wide:
"There are the Apennines, and here the Caucasus!"
Every molehill was a mountain to his eyes.
After some days' travel, the creature came
to a certain district where upon the shore
Thetis had deposited a great bed of oysters.
And our rat, at his first sight, assumed
the shellfish were a fleet of ships.
"What a pathetic figure my father cut,"
he mused, "never daring to see the world,
timid to the last. Now I have seen the sea,
crossed deserts, though without a drop to drink."
The rat had acquired this information, so to speak,
from a certain professor, and spoke as he ran,
not being one of those rats who, chewing books,
become thereby knowledgeable to the teeth!
Among so many tight-shut oysters there was one
that lay open, gaping in the sunshine,
flattered by a gentle breeze, and taking
the air as if it asked for nothing better:
white, plump, and evidently of matchless savor.
No sooner had the rat caught sight of this
yawning bivalve than he exclaimed (to himself):

"What do I see? It is some delicacy—and if
the color of the creature does not deceive me,
today (or never) I shall dine gastronomically!"
Thereupon our rat, filled with eager hope,
approached the gaping shell, stuck out his
neck, and thereupon was caught fast, as in a trap,
for the oyster straightway closed fast upon
the victim of his own ignorance, the rat.

This fable affords more than one moral—
first of all we discern that those who have
no experience of the world are astonished
by the merest trifles, and then we may learn
how potential captors may themselves be caught.

—LA FONTAINE

translated by Richard Howard

Prodigal

A boy took a slate from a student at school and brought it home to his mother. Instead of beating him as he expected, she praised him. Then he stole a coat and showed it to her. Again she praised him. When he grew older he fell in with a band of thieves and murderers. One day legionnaires caught him riding a stolen donkey, blood on his hands, a merchant's gold in his pockets. He was led through the town square to the executioner's block with his arms tied behind him. Men spat at him; children poked him with sticks. His mother ran behind him, wailing, clawing her breasts. The young man told his jailers, "Please, I want to whisper something to my mother." The jailers held back the crowd, and as his mother came up to him, he took hold of her ear with his teeth and bit it. Then he hissed, "Mother, praise me now."

—AESOP

adapted by Jerome Charyn

Fable of the Man and of the God of the Wodes

Of the euylle man somtyme prouffiteth somme other/ he doth hit not by his good wylle/ but by force/ As reherceth to vs this fable/ Of a man whiche had in his hows an ydolle the whiche oftyme he adoured as his god/ to whome ofte he prayd that he wold gyue to hym moche good And the more that he prayd hym/ the more he faylled/ and became pouere/ wherfore the man was wel wrothe ageynst his ydolle/ and took hit by the legges/ and smote the hede of hit so strongly ageynst the walle/ so that it brake in to many pyeces/ Oute of the whiche ydolle yssued a ryght grete tresoure/ wherof the man was ful gladde and Ioyous/ And thenne the man sayd to his ydolle/ Now knowe I wel/ that thou art wycked/ euyl and peruers/ For whanne I haue wor-shipped the/ thow hast not holpen me/ And now whanne I haue bete the/ thow hast moche done for me/ ¶And therfore the euylle man whanne he doth ony good/ it is not of his good wylle/ but by force/

—WILLIAM CAXTON

The Tiger and the Persimmon

One night a tiger came down to a village. It crept stealthily into the garden of a house and listened at the window. It heard a child crying. Then came the voice of its mother scolding it. "Stop crying this very minute! The tiger is here!" But the child took no notice and went on crying. So the tiger said to himself, "The child is not the least bit afraid of me. He must be a real hero." Then the mother said, "Here is a dried persimmon." And the child stopped crying immediately. Now the tiger was really frightened and said to himself, "This persimmon must be a terrible creature." And it gave up its plan of carrying off the child.

So it went to the outhouse to get an ox instead. There was a thief in there, and he mistook it for an ox and got on its back. The tiger was terrified, and ran off as fast as it could go. "This must be the terrible persimmon attacking me!" it thought. The thief still rode on its back and whipped it up so that he might get away before the villagers saw him stealing an ox.

When it grew light the thief saw he was riding on a tiger and leapt off. But the tiger just raced on to the mountains without looking back.

—KOREA

as told by Ma He-Song

The Fox

The fox having urinated into the sea said, "The whole of the sea is my urine."

—Sumer

translated by Ben Edwin Perry

The Blue Jackal

There was once a jackal named Fierce-Howl, who lived in a cave near the suburbs of a city. One day he was hunting for food, his throat pinched with hunger, and wandered into the city after nightfall. There the city dogs snapped at his limbs with their sharp-pointed teeth, and terrified his heart with their dreadful barking, so that he stumbled this way and that in his efforts to escape and happened into the house of a dyer. There he tumbled into a tremendous indigo vat, and all the dogs went home.

Presently the jackal—further life being predestined —managed to crawl out of the indigo vat and escaped into the forest. There all the thronging animals in his vicinity caught a glimpse of his body dyed with the juice of indigo, and crying out: "What is this creature enriched with that unprecedented color?" they fled, their eyes dancing with terror, and spread the report: "Oh, oh! Here is an exotic creature that has dropped from somewhere. Nobody knows what his conduct might be, or his energy. We are going to vamoose. For the proverb says:

> Where you do not know
> Conduct, stock, and pluck,
> 'Tis not wise to trust,
> If you wish for luck."

Now Fierce-Howl perceived their dismay, and called to them: "Come, come, you wild things! Why do you flee in terror at sight of me? For Indra, realizing that the forest creatures have no monarch, anointed me—my name is Fierce-Howl—as your king. Rest in safety within the cage formed by my resistless paws."

On hearing this, the lions, tigers, leopards, monkeys, rabbits, gazelles, jackals, and other species of wild life bowed humbly, saying: "Master, prescribe to us our duties." Thereupon he appointed the lion prime minister and the tiger lord of the bedchamber, while the leopard was made custodian of the king's betel, the elephant doorkeeper, and the monkey the bearer of the royal parasol. But to all the jackals, his own kindred, he administered a cuffing, and drove them away. Thus he enjoyed the kingly glory, while lions and others killed food-animals and laid them before him. These he divided and distributed to all after the manner of kings.

While time passed in this fashion, he was sitting one day in his court when he heard the sound made by a pack of jackals howling near by. At this his body thrilled, his eyes filled with tears of joy, he leaped to his feet, and began to howl in a piercing tone. When the lions and others heard this, they perceived that he was a jackal, and stood for a moment shamefaced and downcast, then they said: "Look! We have been deceived by this jackal. Let the fellow be killed." And when he heard this, he endeavored to flee, but was torn to bits by a tiger and died.

—from *The Panchatantra*
translated by Arthur W. Ryder

Nightingale and Bat

As a caged nightingale was singing one night, a bat flapped at the window in which she hung, and asked her why she is still during the day but so sweet-sounding at night. I was caught, said the nightingale, singing in the light; so as a precaution I keep quiet till it's dark. You should have thought of it then, answered the other; for as it is now, you're in no danger of being snapped singing again.

—MEDIEVAL AESOPICA and ROGER L'ESTRANGE

composite by Karen Kennerly

A Lion and an Asse

An *Asse* was so Hardy once, as to fall a Mopping and Braying at a *Lyon*. The *Lyon* began at first to shew his Teeth, and to Stomack the Affront; but upon Second Thoughts; Well! (says he) *Jeer on, and be an* ASSE *still*. Take notice only by the way, that 'tis the Baseness of your Character that has sav'd your Carcass.

The MORAL: *It is below the Dignity of a Great Mind to Entertain Contests with People that have neither Quality or Courage: Beside the Folly of Contending with a Miserable Wretch, where the very Competition is a Scandel.*

—ROGER L'ESTRANGE

Beans and Husks

The holy man of Shosha accumulated so much merit by frequent reading aloud of the Lotus Sutra that his sixth sense attained a state of purity. Once while on a journey, he entered an inn and heard the murmur of beans as they were boiled over a fire of bean husks. The beans were saying, "How cruel of you, who have been so close to us, to subject us to this terrible ordeal of boiling!" The husks made a crackling sound as they burnt which, the holy man could tell, meant, "Do you suppose we like doing it? Being burnt is horribly painful, but there is nothing we can do to prevent it. Don't be angry with us."

—KENKŌ   (from *Essays in Idleness*)
translated by Donald Keene

The Wounded Pine Tree

Some woodmen, after splitting a tough pine partway, put wedges in it to pry it apart and make their work thereafter easier. The pine tree groaned and said: "How could I blame the axe so much, which was no kin of mine, as these vile wedges of which I am the mother? Inserted in me here and there they will rend me apart."

This truth the myth reveals to all of us: nothing that one may suffer from outsiders is so terrible as what one suffers by the work of one's own kin.

—BABRIUS

translated by Ben Edwin Perry

The Mice That Ate Iron

In a certain town lived a merchant named Naduk, who lost his money and determined to travel abroad. For

The meanest of mankind is he
Who, having lost his money, can
Inhabit lands or towns where once
He spent it like a gentleman.

And again:

The neighbor gossips blame
His poverty as shame
Who long was wont to play
Among them, proud and gay.

In his house was an iron balance-beam inherited from his ancestors, and it weighed a thousand *pals*. This he put in pawn with Merchant Lakshman before he departed for foreign countries.

Now after he had long traveled wherever business led him through foreign lands, he returned to his native city and said to Merchant Lakshman: "Friend Lakshman, return my deposit, the balance-beam." And Lakshman said: "Friend Naduk, your balance-beam has been eaten by mice."

To this Naduk replied: "Lakshman, you are in no way to blame, if it has been eaten by mice. Such is life. Nothing in the universe has any permanence. However,

I am going to the river for a bath. Please send your boy Money-God with me, to carry my bathing things."

Since Lakshman was conscience-stricken at his own theft, he said to his son Money-God: "My dear boy, let me introduce Uncle Naduk, who is going to the river to bathe. You must go with him and carry his bathing things." Ah, there is too much truth in the saying:

> There is no purely loving deed
> Without a pinch of fear or greed
> Or service of a selfish need.

And again:

> Wherever there is fond attention
> That does not seek a service pension,
> Was there no timid apprehension?

So Lakshman's son took the bathing things and delightedly accompanied Naduk to the river. After Naduk had taken his bath, he thrust Lakshman's son Money-God into a mountain cave, blocked the entrance with a great rock, and returned to Lakshman's house. And when Lakshman said: "Friend Naduk, tell me what has become of my son Money-God who went with you," Naduk answered: "My good Lakshman, a hawk carried him off from the river-bank."

"Oh, Naduk!" cried Lakshman. "You liar! How could a hawk possibly carry off a big boy like Money-God?" "But, Lakshman," retorted Naduk, "the mice could eat a balance-beam made of iron. Give me my balance-beam, if you want your son."

Finally, they carried their dispute to the palace gate, where Lakshman cried in a piercing tone: "Help! Help! A ghastly deed! This Naduk person has carried off my son—his name is Money-God."

Thereupon the magistrates said to Naduk: "Sir, restore the boy to Lakshman." But Naduk pleaded: "What am I to do? Before my eyes a hawk carried him from the river-bank." "Come, Naduk!" said they, "you are not telling the truth. How can a hawk carry off a fifteen-year-old boy?" Then Naduk laughed outright and said: "Gentlemen, listen to my words.

> Where mice eat balance-beams of iron
> A thousand *pals* in weight,
> A hawk might steal an elephant;
> A boy is trifling freight."

"How was that?" they asked, and Naduk told them the story of the balance-beam. At this they laughed and caused the restoration of balance-beam and boy to the respective owners.

—from *The Panchatantra*
translated by Arthur W. Ryder

The Bottle-Bird and the Monkey

At the beginning of the rains, a bottle-bird taunted a monkey: "Why didn't you build yourself a house before the rainy season? Your hands and feet are like a man's—you could have made a most useful shelter. The rains will last four months and you will be wet the whole time. It is stupid of you not to have built a house." The monkey got angry. And climbing up to where the bottle-bird's nest was hanging from its branch like a lady's purse, he pulled it down with his hands, and tore it to pieces.

—INDIA

🐫 A Camel at First Sight

Upon the first sight of a *Camel*, all people ran away from't, in amazement at so *Monstrous* a bulk. Upon the second sight, finding that it did them no Hurt, they took Heart upon't, went up to't, and view'd it. But when they came, upon further *Experience*, to take notice, how stupid a *Beast* it was, they ty'd it up, bridled it, loaded it with packs and burdens; set Boys upon the *Back* on't, and treated it with the last degree of *Contempt*.

The MORAL: *Novelty surprises us, and we have naturally a Horror for uncouth misshapen Monsters; but 'tis our Ignorance that staggers us, for upon Custom and Experience, all these Buggs grow familiar, and easy to us.*

—ROGER L'ESTRANGE

The Foxes

At a certain place there was a family of foxes. They were very hungry, and the old fox went off stealing. Late in the evening he returned and said to his wife, "I tried to find a seal-hole and got the scent of one. But whenever I ran with my nose along the ice, I lost it; yet as soon as I raised my head I caught it again in the wind." He asked his wife to make foot-protectors for the young foxes and early the next day they started. They ran with their noses pointed up, and soon found the scent was that of a dead whale which was locked in the ground ice. They went right inside the whale and were well supplied, living in a house that was all meat.

One day they saw a number of wolves coming. The foxes were afraid—they thought the wolves might want to stay there also, to enjoy the whale meat. So the old fox went out and jumped on top of the whale. He shouted to the wolves: "I smell a whale here, but I cannot see it. There are only rocks." The wolves believed the fox and turned away. When they had gone, the fox ran back into the whale and joked: " 'I smell a whale here . . .' "

—Eskimo   (*Baffin Land*)

The Two Monkeys

The learned, full of inward pride,
        The fops of outward show deride;
The fop, with learning at defiance,
Scoffs at the pedant and the science;
The Don, a formal solemn strutter,
Despises Monsieur's airs and flutter;
While Monsieur mocks the formal fool,
Who looks, and speaks, and walks, by rule.
Britain, a medley of the twain,
As pert as France, as grave as Spain,
In fancy wiser than the rest,
Laughs at them both, of both the jest,
Is not the Poet's chiming close,
Censured by all the sons of Prose?
While bards of quick imagination
Despise the sleepy prose narration.
Men laugh at apes, they men contemn;
For what are we, but apes to them?
        Two Monkeys went to Southwark fair,
No critics had a sourer air:
They forced their way through draggled folks,
Who gaped to catch Jack Pudding's jokes;
Then took their tickets for the show,
And got by chance the foremost row.
To see their grave observing face
Provok'd a laugh throughout the place.

"Brother," says Pug, and turn'd his head,
"The rabble's monstrously ill-bred."
    Now through the booth loud hisses ran,
Nor ended till the show began.
The tumbler whirls the flip-flap round,
With sommersets he shakes the ground;
The cord beneath the dancer springs;
Aloft in air the vaulter swings;
Distorted now, now prone depends,
Now through his twisted arms ascends;
The crowd, in wonder and delight,
With clapping hands applaud the sight.
    With smiles, quoth Pug, "If pranks like these
The giant apes of reason please,
How would they wonder at our arts?
They must adore us for our parts.
High on the twig I've seen you cling,
Play, twist, and turn in airy ring:
How can those clumsy things like me
Fly with a bound from tree to tree?
But yet, by this applause, we find
These emulators of our kind
Discern our worth, our parts regard,
Who our mean mimics thus reward."
    "Brother," the grinning mate replies,
"In this I grant that man is wise,
While good example they pursue,
We must allow some praise is due;
But when they strain beyond their guide,
I laugh to scorn the mimic pride;

For how fantastic is the sight,
To meet men always bolt upright,
Because we sometimes walk on two!
I hate the imitating crew."

—JOHN GAY

The Astonishing Pigeon

A sharp pigeon, his pink and yellow silk tie fluttering back over his natty tailfeathers, flew up high over the Empire State Building in New York City. Once he was in good position, he looked down at the skyscrapers of Manhattan, unstrapped a bright red megaphone from his right leg, and shouted into it: "Tomorrow, at twelve noon, I will set the sea on fire." Everyone looked up. Soon the TV crews were on the scene, and the pigeon's picture was shown from coast to coast as the newscasters said, "Tomorrow, this pigeon will set the sea on fire." They went on to talk about baseball games and stock prices, but no one listened to them. The news went everywhere. Even the fish heard about it, and worried: "Our goose might be cooked," they said, "or is it our fish?" All the people from their apartments and houses, and the birds from their trees, and the squirrels from the parks, rushed to the shore the next day to see the ocean burn and bubble. "This is gonna be boss," said one fat squirrel. "Fantastic, fantastic, fantastic," said a blue jay. "Rather interesting," said a human being, with glasses on his nose. Some people even knelt down by the water, spoons in their hands, to see what kind of soup the ocean would make, once it boiled up enough. The clocks struck twelve and everyone became quiet, their eyes wide, staring at the waves. "There it goes, man, it's boiling," said the squirrel, but the sea was as cold as ever. "If it would just bubble it would be fantastic," said the blue jay, but the sea was cold as ever. "Nothing is happening," said the man with glasses on his nose.

And how did the pigeon's plan end up? He took off as fast as he could, his gay tie drooping from his neck, his face as red as a pigeon's face can get. Everyone hissed, and booed, and laughed. The sea was cold as ever, and the pigeon was so famous that he didn't dare show his face to pick up his share of popcorn in the park.

—LEONARD JENKIN

A Salmon and a Dog-Fish

I prithee, who is greatest? can you tell?
  Sad tales befit my woe: I'll tell you one.
A salmon, as she swam unto the sea,
Met with a dog-fish, who encounters her
With this rough language: 'Why art thou so bold
To mix thyself with our high state of floods,
Being no eminent courtier, but one
That for the calmest and fresh time o' the year
Dost live in shallow rivers, rank'st thyself
With silly smelts and shrimps? and darest thou
Pass by our dogship without reverence?'
'Oh,' quoth the salmon, 'sister, be at peace:
Thank Jupiter we both have pass'd the net!
Our value never can be truly known,
Till in the fisher's basket we be shown:
I' the market then my price may be the higher,
Even when I am nearest to the cook and fire.'
So to great men the moral may be stretch'd;
Men oft are valu'd high, when they're most wretch'd.

—JOHN WEBSTER

Coyote and His Wife

Coyote had Toad for a wife. He beat her so regularly that she had warts on her back. So at nights Coyote would creep away looking for new girls.

One evening he heard of a dance a long way off. Under the pretext of hunting, Coyote went and danced, and saw a girl all painted up. This excited him. He sang a song asking her to be his partner. They danced together, and made love behind the bushes.

In the morning Coyote woke and saw that the girl was Toad. He felt miserably tricked: Coyote beat Toad so much that her wrists became limber.

—WINTU (*California*)

A Physician That Cur'd Mad-Men

There was a Physician in *Milan* that took upon him to Cure Mad-men; and his way was this: They were Ty'd Naked to a Stake, and then set up right in a Nasty Puddle, Deeper or Shallower, according to the degree of the Distemper; and there to continue, till betwixt Cold and Hunger they might be brought to their Wits again. There was one among the rest, that after Fifteen Days Soking, began to shew some signs of Amendment; and so got leave of the Keeper for the Liberty of the Court, and the House, upon condition not to set Foot over the Threshold of the Street-Doors. He past his Promise, and was as good as his Word.

As he was standing one Day at the Outer-Gate, there came a *Falkner* Riding by, with his Kites and his Curs, and all his *Hawking Trade* about him. Heark ye Sir, says the Mad-Man, a word with you: And so he fell to asking him Twenty Idle Questions, What was *this*, and what was *that*, and 'tother? And what was all this *good* for? and the like. The Gentleman gave him an Answer to every thing in Form. As for Example, *This that I Ride upon*, (says he) *is a* Horse, *that I keep for my Sport*; *this Bird upon my Fist is a* Hawk *that Catches me Quails and Partridges*; *and those Dogs are* Spaniels *to spring my Game*. That's well, says the Fool, and what may all the Birds be worth now, that you catch in a Twelve Month? Why it may be some *Ten or Fifteen Pound* perhaps, says 'tother. Ay but (says the Mad Fellow again,) what may all your *Hawks, Dogs,* and *Horses* cost you in a Year?

Some Fifteen times as much perchance, says the *Falkner.* Get you out of the way then immediately (cries the Fool,) before our Doctor gets sight of you; for if he sowc'd me up to the Middle in the Pond, you'll be in as sure as a Gun up to the Ears if he can but set Eye on ye.

—ROGER L'ESTRANGE

The Dolls

A Doll in the doll-maker's house
    Looks at the cradle and bawls:
'That is an insult to us.'
But the oldest of all the dolls,
Who had seen, being kept for show,
Generations of his sort,
Out-screams the whole shelf: 'Although
There's not a man can report
Evil of this place,
The man and woman bring
Hither, to our disgrace,
A noisy and filthy thing.'
Hearing him groan and stretch
The doll-maker's wife is aware
Her husband has heard the wretch,
And crouched by the arm of his chair,
She murmurs into his ear,
Head upon shoulder leant:
"My dear, my dear, O dear,
It was an accident.'

—WILLIAM BUTLER YEATS

The Rich Man of Sung

Once there was a rich man of Sung. When the dirt wall around his house collapsed in a heavy rain, his son said, "If you don't rebuild it, thieves will surely break in," and the old man who lived next door told him the same thing. When night fell, thieves actually broke in and made off with a large share of the rich man's wealth. The rich man's family praised the son for his wisdom, but eyed the old man next door with suspicion.

—HAN FEI TZU

translated by Burton Watson

Mountain in Labor

A Mountain, for her labor braced,
  Let out a shout so wondrous wild
That one and all raced up in haste,
Supposed they'd behold a child
As big as Paris' enceinte, or more;
But no, a Mouse was what she bore.

—LA FONTAINE
translated by Francis Duke

The Clod and the Pebble

Love seeketh not Itself to please,
    "Nor for itself hath any care,
"But for another gives its ease,
"And builds a Heaven in Hell's despair."

So sang a little Clod of Clay
Trodden with the cattle's feet,
But a Pebble of the brook
Worbled out these metres meet:

"Love seeketh only Self to please,
"To bind another to its delight,
"Joys in another's loss of ease,
"And builds a Hell in Heaven's despite."

—WILLIAM BLAKE

The Glow-Worm

A Glow-Worm lying in the garden saw a candle flare in a neighboring palace and bemoaned the littleness of his own light. But another next to him observed: Wait; it will soon be dark. I have outlasted many of these glaring lights which brighten most as they haste to nothing.

—from an unfinished fable found in
James Boswell's *Life of Johnson*
adapted by Karen Kennerly

Skunk and His Family

Skunk was disabled and lived all by himself with the burden of his family. So he decided to pretend to die. His wife then called in their friend Buffalo to give her husband a proper burial. Buffalo came, and buried him with his buttocks pointed up from the grave which was the custom in those parts. As they were about to leave the spot, Skunk-woman, weeping, asked Buffalo to kiss Skunk for the last time. Buffalo bent down to caress his friend when Skunk discharged in Buffalo's face, and killed him. Skunk and his family had plenty to eat for a long time.

—SIOUX   (*Iowa*)

You Are Too Kind

A hunter not overbold, trailing a lion
     in mountain forests deep and shady,
came on a woodcutter near a tall pine.

"May the nymphs be nice to you," said he,
"that lion who lives here, have you seen his tracks?"

And the man said:
          "Lucky you came just now;
in half a minute I'll show you the beast himself."

The hunter's face paled and his molars clacked.

"No m-more favors than I ask for, please:
just tell me where the tracks are, not the lion."

—BABRIUS

translated by Robert Fitzgerald

The Fable of the Wulf and of the Dogge

Lyberte or fredome is a moche swete thynge/ as Esope reherceth by this fable/ of a wulf and of a dogge whiche by aduenture mette to gyder/ wherfore the wulf demaunded of the dogge/ wherof arte thow so fatte and so playsaunt/ And the dogge ansuerd to hym/ I haue wel kepte my lordes hows/ & haue barked after the theues whiche came in the hows of my mayster/ wherfore he and his meyny gyue to me plente of good mete/ wherof I am fatte and playsaunt/ and the wulf sayd thenne to hym/ It is wel sayd my broder/ Certaynly syth thow arte so wel atte thyn ease and farest so wel I haue grete desyre to dwelle with the/ to thende that thow & I make but one dyner/ wel sayd the dogge/ come on with me yf thow wylt be as wel at thyn ease as I am/ and haue thou no doubte of no thynge/ The wulf wente with the dogge/ and as they wente by the way/ the wulf beheld the dogges neck/ whiche was al bare of here/ and demaunded of the dogge/ My broder why is thy neck so shauen/ And the dogge ansuerd/ it is by cause of my grete coler of yron/ to the whiche dayly I am fasted/ And at nyght I am vnbound for to kepe the hows the better/ Thenne sayd the wulf to the dogge/ This I myster ne nede not/ For I that am in lyberte/ wylle not be put in so subiection/ And therfor for to fylle my bely/ I wylle not be subget/ yf thou be acustommed for to be bound/ contynue thow

in hit/ and I shalle lyue as I am wonte and acustomed/
therfore there is no rychesse gretter/ than lyberte/ For
lyberte is better than alle the gold of the world/

—WILLIAM CAXTON

A Very Real Story

I t happened that a gentleman dropped his glasses on the floor, which when they hit the tiles, made a terrible noise. The gentleman stoops down to pick them up, very dejected, as the lenses are very expensive, but he discovers with astonishment that by some miracle he hasn't broken them.

Now this gentleman feels profoundly thankful and understands that what has happened amounts to a friendly warning, in such a way that he walks down to an optician's shop and immediately acquires a leather glasses case, padded and double-protected, an ounce of prevention is worth a pound of, etc. An hour later the case falls, and stooping down to recover it without any great anxiety, he discovers that the glasses are in smithereens. It takes this gentleman a while to understand that the designs of Providence are inscrutable, and that in reality the miracle has just now occurred.

—JULIO CORTÁZAR
translated by Paul Blackburn

A Fable with a Still Moral

Who came first—time or the clock? "I," said time; "I," said the clock; and they flew round in a lively debate.

Man was called in to decide, and chose to honor both: so he stepped out of life; and the combatants, to mourn him, concluded fast, and stopped. Thus Peace won out, and was well rid of all three.

—MARVIN COHEN

The Black Marten

There was a tanner who kept a white marten. This marten dined regularly and modestly on one mouse a day. Once, when feeling sleek and satiated he was padding round the rim of a pot of black dye, and slipped: he turned permanently black. The mice assumed that such an extraordinary change in color must also bring about a change in personality; they logically deduced he was no longer carnivorous. Drunk with abandonment, they ran over the floor, sniffing for food and deliberating fastidiously over each morsel they found. The marten was so amazed at the abundance of prey that he neglected at first to pounce, but eventually did manage to swipe at two. In a panic the rest scratched back into their holes, perplexed at how such a mismatch of color and character could be.

—AESOP (*Medieval Prose Polyglot*)
adapted from Lloyd W. Daley's translation by Karen Kennerly

Fox

ABear was living with a Fox. They made a sledge and dragged each other along. First the Bear dragged the Fox, but he got tired. So afterward the Fox dragged the Bear, but he ran into a narrow place between some trees. The Bear screamed, "You are frightful! Where the trees grow thick, do not run so fast." But the Fox did not listen to him. Soon they came to a cliff; the Fox upset the sledge, and the Bear rolled over and was killed. The Fox skinned him, took him home, and ate his meat. When he had finished eating, he tied the bladder to his tail.

Soon the Fox felt hungry again, so he went to the seashore to look for food. He saw a herd of reindeer and one of them said, "Listen, Fox! How did you get such a thing tied to your tail?" "Let me stand among you," answered the Fox, "and if you butt at me with your antlers, you also will have such things attached to your tails." Two reindeer took the Fox between them, and tried to toss him with their antlers; but the Fox leaped away, and they only tangled, and broke against each other. The Fox skinned them and carried home their meat.

—AINU (*Northern Japan*)

🕷 All Stories Are Anansi's

In de beginnin, all tales and stories dey de property of Nyame, de Sky God. But Kwaku Anansi, de spider, he itching to be owner of all de stories known in de world, an he take hisself to Nyame an he offer to buy dem.

De Sky God he say: "I's sweet on selling dese stories, but man, de price too high. Many people come to me offering to buy, but de price too high for dem. De rich an powerful families dey not able to pay. Yuh think yuh can do it?"

Anansi he reply to de Sky God, "Sure I can do it. What's yo price?"

"Me price is three thing," de Sky God say. "I gotto first get Mmoboro, de hornets, I gotto den get Onini, de great python. I gotto den get Osebo de leopard. Fo dese thing, man, I going sell you de title to all de stories."

Anansi say: "Man, I goin bring dem."

Den he take hisself home an make he plans. He first cut a gourd from a vine and chook* a lil hole in it. Den he take a large calabash and fill it with water. He den take hisself to de tree where de hornets stay. He pour some o de water over hisself, so dat he be dripping. He throw some water over de hornets so dat they be dripping too. Then he put de calabash on he head, like he goin protect hisself from a rain, and call out to de hornets: "Man you sure be schupid people. Why yuh stay in de rain when it falling?"

* bore

278:

De hornets dey say: "Where we goin go?"

"Go here man, in dis dry gourd," Anansi say.

De hornets dey thank him an fly into dis gourd through de lil hole. When de last of dem done enter, Anansi he plug up de hole with a ball of grass, saying: "Man, you sure schupid people!"

Him take de gourd fill up with hornets to Nyame, de Sky God. De Sky God he accept dem. Him say: "Man, you has two more thing to get."

Anansi he go back to de bushes an he cut a long bamboo stick an some strong vines. Then he walk up round de house of Onini, de python, making conversation with hisself. Him say: "Me woman schupid. I say him longer and stronger, her say him shorter and weaker. I gives him more due. Her give him less due. Who right? Me soul* or me? I right him is longer. I right, him is stronger."

When Onini de python, he hear Anansi making conversation with hisself, he say: "Man, why yuh fussing so with yuhself?"

De spider he reply: "Man, I done has dis ruckus with me woman. She say yuh is shorter an weaker than dis bamboo stick. I say yuh longer an stronger."

Onini say: "It sure useless and silly you be fussing with yuhself to find out de truth. Bring de stick an we goin count."

So Anansi he done put down de stick on de ground, and de python he come and stretch hisself out beside it.

"You seem a lil short," Anansi say.

De python, man, he stretch some more.

* wife

"A lil more," Anansi say.

"Me noh can stretch no more," Onini say.

"Man, when you done stretch at one end, you done get shorter at de other end," Anansi say. "I going tie yuh at de front so you don no slip."

Den he tie Onini head to de pole. Den he go back to de other end and he tie de tail to de pole. Den he wrap de vine round Onini, so de python he noh can move.

"Onini," Anansi say, "Man, it turn out me soul she right and I wrong. You sure shorter than de pole an weaker too. Me opinion it not as good as me woman. But yuh sure more schupid than me, an I got you in me power."

Anansi he carry de python to Nyame, de Sky God, and de Sky God he say: "Now you has gotto to get one more thing."

Osebo, de leopard he come next. Anansi he done go back to de bush and he done dig hisself a deep pit where he know de leopard come walking all de time. He cover it with lil branch and leave and he put earth on it, so de leopard he can not see de pit. Den Anansi he leave and go hide. When Osebo come prowling round in de black-o-night, he step into de trap Anansi done prepare and fall to de bottom. Anansi he hear de sound of de leopard fallin an he say: "Man Osebo, yuh sure half-schupid."

When de mawning come, Anansi he done go to de pit and he spy de leopard dere.

"Osebo," he question, "What yuh doin in dis hole, man?"

"I done fall into dis trap," Osebo say, "Man, help me out of it."

"I sure be glad to help you," Anansi say. "But, man, I's sure dat if I takes you out, yuh not goin thank me fo it. Yuh goin get hungry an soon you going be sweet on eating me and me children."

"Man, I done swear to you it not goin be dat way!" Osebo say.

"Well, then, since you done swear it, I has to take you out," Anansi say.

Den he bend de tall green tree till it reach de ground, so de top now over de pit an he tie it up dat way. Then he tie a rope to de top of de tree an he drop de other end of it into de pit.

"Now you gotto tie dis to your tail," he say.

Osebo he tie de rope to his tail.

"It be well tied?" Anansi ask.

"Yes, man, it well tied," de leopard say.

"Well then," Anansi say, "You sure not just half-schupid, you all-schupid."

Den take de blade and cut de other rope, de one holding de tree bowed to de ground. De tree she straighten up with a snap and pull Osebo out of de hole. He hang in de air downward, him twisting and turning. Den while he hang dis way, Anansi come kill him with he weapons.

Den he take de body o de leopard and gon with it to Nyame de Sky God, saying: "Here be de third thing. Now I done Pay me price."

Nyame he say to him: "Kwaku Anansi, great warriors an chief dey try to do dis, but man, dey couldn't do it. You done it. So I going give you de stories. So from den on, all de stories dey belong to you. Whenever somebody tell a story, he got to say dat it be Anansi's tale."

In dis way, Anansi de spider he become de owner of all de stories dat dey tell. Anansi got all de tales in he pocket.

—Trinidadian version of an African tale
adapted by Barbara Christian

Fable of the Wulf
and of the Hongry Dogge

S vche supposen somtyme to wynne that lesen/ As hit
appiereth by this Fable/ For hit is sayd comunly/
that as moche dispendeth the nygard as the large/ As
hit appiereth by this Fable of a man whiche had a grete
herd of sheep/ And also he had a dogge for to kepe them
fro the wulues/ To this dogge he gaf no mete/ for the
grete auaryce whiche held hym/ And therfore the wulf
on a daye came to the dogge/ and demaunded of hym
the rayson/ why he was soo lene/ and sayd to hym/ I see
wel that thow dyest for honger/ by cause that thy mayster
gyueth to the no mete/ by his grete scarcyte/ but yf thow
wylt byleue me I shalle gyue to the good counceylle/ And
the dogge sayd to hym/ Certaynly I myster gretely of good
counceylle/   ¶Thenne the wulf sayd to hym/ This
shalt thow doo/ Lete me take a lambe/ And whanne I
shalle haue hit I shalle renne awey/ And whanne
thow shalt see me renne/ make thenne semblaunt to
renne after me/ and lete thy self falle faynynge that thow
canst not ouertake me/ for lack and fawte of mete/ which
maketh the so feble/ And thus whanne the sheepherd
shalle see that thow mayst not haue the lambe fro me by
cause of the grete feblenesse and debylyte of thy lene
body/ he shall telle to thy lord that thow myghtest not
socoure the lambe/ by cause that thow arte so sore ahon-
gryd/ and by this meane thow shalt haue mete thy bely
ful/   ¶The dogge thenne acorded this with the
wulf/ and eche of them made and dyde as aboue is sayd/

¶And whanne the sheepherd sawe the dogge falle/ supposed wel/ that honger was cause of it For the whiche cause whanne one of the sheepherdes came home he told hit to his mayster/ And whan the mayster vnderstood hit/ he seyd as a man wroth for shame/ I wylle that fro hensforthon he haue breed ynough/ ¶And thenne euery daye the sayd dogge hadde soppes of brede/ and of drye breed he hadde ynough/ ¶Thenne the dogge toke strengthe/ and vygour ageyne/ ¶It happed within a lytyl whyle after/ that the wulf came ageyne to the dogge/ and sayd to hym/ I perceyue wel/ that I gaf to the good-counceylle/ And the dogge sayd to the wulf/ My broder thow sayst soothe/ wherfore I thanke the moche/ For of hit I hadde grete nede/

¶And thenne the wulf sayd to hym/ Yf thow wylt I shall gyue to the yet better counceylle/ And the dogge ansuerd hym with ryght a good wylle I shalle here hit/ And yf hit be good I shalle doo after hit/ ¶Thenne sayd the wulf to hym Lete me take yet another lambe/ and doo thy dylygence for to haue hit fro me/ and to byte me/ and I shalle ouerthrowe the thy feet vpward/ as he that hath no puyssaunce ne strength withoute hurtynge of thy self/ byleue me hardyly/ and wel hit shalle happe to the/ And whanne thy maysters seruaunts shalle haue sene thy dylygence/ they shalle shewe hit to thy mayster how that thow shalt kepe full wel his folde/ yf thou be wel nourysshed/ ¶And thenne the dogge ansuerd 'to the wulf that he was contente/ And as hit was sayd/ ryght so hit was done/ and bothe of them maad good dylygence The wulf bare aweye the lambe/ and the dogge ranne after hym/ and ouertook hym/ & bote hym fayntly/ And the wulf ouerthrewe the dogge vpso-

doune to the ground/ And whan the sheepherdes sawe
gyue suche strokes amonge the dogge & the wulf/ sayd
Certaynly we haue a good dogge/ we muste telle his
dylygence to our mayster/ and soo they dyd/ & how he
bote the wulf/ and how he was ouerthrowen/ and yet
sayd Certaynly yf he hadde hadde euer mete ynough/
the wulf had not borne awey the lambe/ Thenne the lord
commaunded to gyue hym plente of mete/ wherof the
dogge took ageyne al strengthe and vertue/ And within
a whyle after the wulf came ageyne to the dogge/ and
sayd to hym in this manere/ My broder haue I not gyuen
to the good counceylle/ And thenne the dogge ansuerd
to hym/ Certaynly ye/ wherof I thanke yow/ And the
wulf sayd to the dogge/ I praye the my broder and my
good frend that thow wylt yet gyue another lambe/ and
the dogge sayd to hym/ Certaynly my broder/ wel hit
maye suffyse the to haue had tweyne of them/ ¶Thenne
sayd the wulf to the dogge/ ¶At the lest waye I maye haue
one for my laboure and sallarye/ That shalt thow not
haue sayd the dogge/ Hast thow not hadde good sallarye
for to haue hadde two lambes oute of my maysters herd/
¶And the wulf ansuerd to hym ageyne/ My brother gyue
hit me yf hit please the/ ¶And after sayd the dogge to
hym/ Nay I wylle not/ And yf thow takest hit ageynste
my wylle/ I promytte and warne the/ that neuer after
this tyme thow shalt ete none/ And thenne the wulf sayd
to hym/ Allas my broder I deye for honger/ Counceylle
me for goddys loue what I shalle doo/ And the dogge sayd
to hym/ I shal counceylle the wel a walle of my maysters
celer is fallen doune/ go thyeer this nyght and entre in
hit/ and there thow mayst both ete and drynke after thy
playsyr/ For bothe breed flesshe and wyn shalt thow fynde

at plente there within/ And thenne the wulf sayd to hym/ Allas my broder/ beware wel thenne/ that thow accuse ne deceyue me not/ And the dogge ansuerd/ I waraunt the/ but doo thy faytte soo pryuely/ that none of my felawes knowe not of hit/ ¶And the wulf came at the nyght/ and entryd in to the celer/ and/ ete and dranke at his playsyre/ In so moche that he wexed dronk/ And whanne he hadde dronke soo moche/ that he was dronke/ He sayd to hym self/ whanne the vylaynes ben fylled wyth metes/ and that they ben dronke/ they synge theyr songes/ and I wherfore shold I not synge/ ¶And thenne he beganne to crye and to howle/ And the dogges herd the voys of hym wherfore they beganne to barke and to howle/ And the servaunts whiche herd them sayd/ It is the wulf/ whiche is entryd within the celer/ And thenne they al to gyder wenten thyder/ and kylled the wulf/ And therfore more dispendeth the nygard than the large/ For maryec was neuer good/ For many one ben whiche dare not ete ne drynke is nature requyreth/ But neuertheles euery one oughte to vse and lyue prudently of alle suche goodes as god sendeth to hym/ This fable also shew it to vs/ that none ought to do ageynste his kynde/ as of the wulf whiche waxed dronke/ for the whiche cause he was slayne

—WILLIAM CAXTON

The Image

I saw an Image, all of massie gold,
 Placed on high vpon an Altare faire,
That all, which did the same from farre beholde,
Might worship it, and fall on lowest staire.
Not that great Idoll might with this compaire,
To which th' *Assyrian* tyrant would haue made
The holie brethren falslie to haue praid.

But th' Altare, on the which this Image staid,
Was (O great pitie) built of brickle clay,
That shortly the foundation decaid,
With showers of heauen and tempests worne away:
Then downe it fell, and low in ashes lay,
Scorned of euerie one, which by it went;
That I it seing, dearelie did lament.

—EDMUND SPENSER

The Owl and the Two Rabbits

An Owl spotted two Rabbits playing close together and seized them, one clutched in each foot. But they were too strong for him and ran away, sliding the Owl along the ice. The Owl's wife shouted to him, "Let one of them go and kill the other!" But he replied, "The Moon will soon disappear, and then we shall be hungry. We need both of them." The Rabbits ran on; and when they came to a boulder, one ran to the right side of it, the other to the left. The Owl did not let go quick enough, and was torn in two.

—Eskimo

The Dove and the Fox

A dove was sitting on a cross. A fox passed below and saw him. He spoke aloud and said to him, "Why do you sit up there in so strong a wind? Now, come down and sit beside me in shelter."

"I do not dare," he replied.

"You needn't be afraid of me, and I can tell you why. I was recently at an assembly where many people were gathered together. A letter came from the king, who commanded in good faith that no beast should injure another beast or bird. God forbid that war should be between them any more. He desires to have peace in his land; bird and beast will be able to go and play together."

"Now I will descend," said the dove. "But I see yonder near the bushes two horsemen riding quickly, and bringing two dogs with them."

"Are they very near?" said the fox.

"They ride steadily," said he.

"It is better that I go into the wood than have strife or uproar with them. I do not know whether they have heard the letter which came from the King. I assure you that I would not have to leave if they had heard it."

—MARIE DE FRANCE

The Woman and the Jug

PROCLEON.   Listen, don't go away. You know about the
woman from Sybaris who broke a jug?

CITIZEN (to his friend).   I call you to witness.

PROCLEON.   That's exactly what the jug did. It called a
friend to witness. And the woman said, "If you spent
less time calling people to witness, and went out and
bought a rivet, you'd be showing more sense."

—ARISTOPHANES   (from *The Wasps*)

translated by David Barrett

Woodpecker and the Toad*

Once, in the dry season, a woodpecker discovered a black honey-comb in the hollow of a tree. While sucking out the sticky meat, he noticed a toad eyeing him from below, so invited him to share his meal. The toad accepted; the woodpecker then lowered a creeper and gave instructions on how the toad should wind it about his belly, that he might be drawn up. But just as he was swaying close to the honey-comb the woodpecker wickedly let go, and the toad splattered to the ground. This trick angered him so much he ran from stream to stream and drank them all, droughting the whole island. The success of his revenge made him deliriously happy: thoughtlessly he began to dance—and all the water flowed out of him and the streams filled again.

—ANDAMAN ISLANDS

* This fable accounts for a legendary drought suffered by the ancestors of the Andaman people.

The Mole

People who claim the impossible are such fools that they are shown up in the simplest things.

A mole—a blind animal—said to his mother, "I see." To test him she gave him a little lump of frankincense and asked him what it was. When he said it was a pebble, his mother replied: "My child, you've not only been denied eyesight, but you don't even possess a sense of smell."

—AESOP   (*Medieval Prose Polyglot*)

slightly adapted from Lloyd W. Daley's translation by
Karen Kennerly

The Moon Begs a New Gown

The *Moon* was in a heavy Twitter once, that her *Cloaths* never Fitted her: Wherefore, Pray Mother, says she, let the Taylor take Measure of me for a *New-Gown*. Alas Child, says the Mother, how is it possible to make any one Garment to Fit a Body that appears every Day in a Several Shape?

—ROGER L'ESTRANGE

Snake and Child

Little baby, crawlin' in the yard, seem to be quite satisfied. Snake, milk snake, must have smelt milk on the child, became very fond of the baby. As the child grew older, would take food out to the snake. One day the mother went an' saw the snake. Screamed, husban' came and killed the snake. Child became very ill, like to die.

—AMERICAN FOLK (*Alabama*)

A Lamb, a Wolf and a Goat

A *Wolf* overheard a *Lamb* Bleating among the *Goats.* D'ye hear Little One, (says the *Wolf,*) if it be your Dam you want, she's yonder in the Field. Ay (says the Lamb,) but I am not looking for her that was my Mother for her *Own* sake, but for her that Nurses me up, and Suckles me out of *Pure Charity,* and *Good Nature.* Can any thing be Dearer to you, says the *Wolf,* then she that brought you forth? Very Right, says the Lamb; and without knowing or caring what she did: And pray, what did she bring me forth *for* too; but to Ease her self of a *Burden,* and to deliver me out of her own Belly, into the Hands of the *Butcher?* I am more Beholden to her that took Pity of me when I was in the World already, then to her that brought me into't, I know not how. 'Tis *Charity,* not *Nature,* or *Necessity* that does the Office of a *Tender Mother.*

The MORAL: *There's a difference betwixt Reverence and Affection; the one goes to the Character, and the other to the Person, and so distinguishes Duty from Inclination.*

—ROGER L'ESTRANGE

♨ The Very Long Tale of an Ass and His Driver

"**A**nd Jesus said, 'A man loaded a statue on his ass and drove it toward the town. As many people met them and did obeisance to the image, the ass supposed that they were bowing to him. He became so puffed up that he would not move a step further. The driver then knew his beast's mind and gave him a thump with his club, saying, 'That's all we needed, you poor fool, for people to bow down to an ass like you.' And Jesus left them, and went within to pray.

"And the disciples had speech, one with the other, asking what the lord had meant by it. Peter spoke first and said, 'It is a tale of a man who thinks other men revere him. The other men are fools, as they worship an idol, and not the true God. He is a fool, as the homage of men can turn his head and make him forget his duty to his driver. This driver is the God of wrath who strikes out with his club of fire, condemning the man to bear his burden of pride onward once more.' And John spoke and said to them, 'Remember that the ass does carry the divine in him, as he carries the statue. Yet the people are not wise in their worship, as it is not yet truly a part of him. He bears it on his back. The driver is God, who reminds him of his lowly state. Note that the driver says "we," and that it is he who has loaded the beast with his burden.' Then Judas, called Iscariot, cried out and said, 'No! The driver is the devil and the ass a true man of God. See the driver's cruelty in loading another with temptation. His fellow demons appear on the road. The holy man pretends to succumb to pride, yet he will not move further toward the town, the stronghold of all temptation. If the driver was all-knowing God, would he need to suddenly know his beast's mind in a situation he himself has created? Does the God of forgiveness thump with clubs? Even after the devil beats him, we get no indication that the holy man moves forward at all. The divine image is surely the image of the ass himself.'

"And Jesus entered again into their midst and said, 'The ass is an ass, the driver a driver, the people people. The road to the town is long, and who knows how many eternities it will take for the ass and the driver to reach their goal, and be forever relieved of their burdens.' "

—LEONARD JENKIN

The Story of the Crocodile

In this country there is a river in the north called the Nile. At one time a large crocodile arrived there. It went everywhere, killing cattle and herdsmen; it even bit travelers. The fear of the people grew. So the chief of the country called an assembly to discuss how the monster might be killed. On the morning of the first session, the fox entered the court. He climbed on a log and spoke: "King and Noblemen, I came to you although I am very small and cannot wrestle with the crocodile. But I can tell you how to avoid such trouble again: You laugh at the crocodile when it is small and weak; but when it is full-grown, you run from it, and are afraid. Crocodiles do not like me much, on account of what I do before they break out of their eggs. I eat them. I can eat fifty in one day. You leave the crocodiles until they are grown. Then you want to be rid of them. No, kill them when they are small."

—VANDAU (*Portuguese South Africa*)

The Cock and the Fox

I tell of a cock that stood on a dunghill and sang. A fox came by and called up to him with fair words. "Sir," he said, "you seem very beautiful to me. I have never seen a bird so finely bred. Your voice is clearer than anything: except your father, whom I knew well, never did bird sing better. But he did better, because he shut his eyes."

"So can I," said the cock. He beat his wings and shut his eyes, thinking to sing more clearly still.

The fox made a jump and grabbed him. Off towards the wood with him he went. In the middle of a field through which he passed the shepherds all ran after him and the dogs barked all round. "Look at the fox! he has taken the cock! There'll be trouble for him, if he comes this way!"

"Go on!" said the cock, "shout back at them. Tell them that I am yours, that you'll never let me go!"

The fox tried to shout at them, and the cock jumped out of his mouth and flew up into a high tree.

When the fox saw his own situation and how he had been badly duped by the cock that had tricked him so cleverly, he fell into a right rage and began to curse that mouth of his which had spoken when it should have kept mum.

The cock replied: "I ought to do the same and curse

those eyes that sought to shut when they should have kept watch and guarded their owner from harm!"

Most fools are just like this. They talk when they should shut up, and shut up when they ought to talk.

—Marie de France

The Wolf on His Deathbed

The Wolf lay in his last agonies, and cast a retrospective glance on his past life. "I am a sinner, that's true," he said. "But still I hope not one of the worst. I have, indeed, done evil, but then I have also done good. For instance, I remember a bleating lamb that once came so near me I could easily have killed it, and I did it no harm. At this time, too, I listened with the most admirable indifference to the jeers and insults of a sheep, where there was no dog near to protect it."

"All this I readily confirm," answered the Fox, who was helping to prepare him for his death. "For I remember all the circumstances of the case. Just at that time, you were choking miserably on a bone caught in your throat, which the kind-hearted crane afterward pulled out."

—G. E. LESSING
translated by James Burns

Story with No Moral

Aman sold cries and words, and he got along all right although he was always running into people who argued about his prices and demanded discounts. The man almost always gave in, and that way he was able to sell a lot of cries to street vendors, a few sighs which ladies on annuities usually bought, and words for fence posters, wall placards, slogans, letterheads, business cards, and used jokes.

The man realized finally that the hour had come and he requested an audience with the dictator of the country, who resembled all his colleagues and received him surrounded by generals, secretaries, and cups of coffee.

"I've come to sell you your last words," the man said. "They are very important because they'll never come out right for you when the moment comes, and on the other hand it would be suitable for you to say them at the critical moment so as in retrospect to shape easily an historical destiny."

"Translate what he's saying," the dictator ordered his interpreter.

"He's speaking Argentine, your Excellency."

"In Argentine? And how come I don't understand it?"

"You have understood very well," the man said. "I repeat, I've come to sell you your final words."

The dictator got to his feet as is the practice under these circumstances, and repressing a shiver ordered that they arrest the man and put him in special dungeons which always exist in those administrative circles.

"It's a pity," said the man while they were leading him off. "In reality you would want to say your final words when the moment arrives, and it would be necessary to say them so as to shape in retrospect, and easily, an historical destiny. What I was going to sell you was what you yourself would want to say, so there's no cheating involved. But as you refuse to do business, you're not going to learn these words beforehand and when the moment arrives when they want to spring out for the first time, naturally you won't be able to say them."

"Why should I not be able to say them if they're what I would have wanted to say anyway?" demanded the dictator, already standing in front of another cup of coffee.

"Because fear will not let you," the man said sadly. "Since there will be a noose around your neck, you'll be in a shirt and shaking in terror and with the cold, your teeth chattering, and you won't be able to articulate a word. The hangman and his assistants, among whom there will be several of these gentlemen, will wait a couple of minutes for decorum's sake, but when your mouth brings forth only a moan interrupted by hiccups and appeals for a pardon (because that, sure, you'll articulate without trouble), they will come to the end of their patience and they'll hang you."

Highly indignant, the assistants and the generals in particular crowded around the dictator to beg that he have the fellow shot immediately. But the dictator, who was-pale-as-death, jostled all of them out the door and shut himself up with the man so as to buy his last words.

The generals and the secretaries in the meantime, humiliated in the extreme by the treatment they had received, plotted an uprising, and the following morning seized the dictator while he was eating grapes in his favorite pavilion. So that he should not be able to say his last words, they shot him then and there, eating grapes. Afterwards they set about to find the man, who had disappeared from the presidential palace, and it didn't take them long to find him since he was walking through the market selling routines to the comedians. Putting him in an armored car they carried him off to the fortress where they tortured him to make him reveal what the dictator's last words would have been. As they could not wring a confession from him, they killed him by kicking him to death.

The street vendors who had bought street cries went on crying them on streetcorners, and one of these cries served much later as the sacred writ and password for the counterrevolution which finished off the generals and the secretaries. Some of them, before their death, thought confusedly that really the whole thing had been a stupid chain of confusions, and that words and cries were things which, strictly speaking, could be sold but could not be bought, however absurd that would seem to be.

And they kept on rotting, the whole lot of them, the dictator, the man, and the generals and the secretaries, but from time to time on streetcorners, the cries could be heard.

—Julio Cortázar
translated by Paul Blackburn

Biographical Notes on the Fabulists

AESOP (Greek fabulist)

Little is known about Aesop, but enough to ascertain that he did exist. He lived in the early sixth century B.C., originally came from Thrace, and was a contemporary of the poet Sappho. In the first part of his life he was a slave on the island of Samos in the service of a man named Iadmon, who later freed him. Most probably he lived out his life on Samos, famed as an inventer and teller of fables, of which he made shrewd use in debates involving conflicts of everyday life. Whether the fables later ascribed to Aesop were the ones he actually told is unknown. Certainly, he never wrote or published. He wasn't a poet, and those books written in prose in sixth-century Greece dealt with historical, philosophical or scientific matters. In those days only poetry was considered literature as such.

ARISTOPHANES (448–388 B.C.) Greek playwright

Nothing is known about the personal life of Aristophanes, except that he had three sons, all of whom were comic poets. He is said to have written fifty-four plays, of which only eleven are extant. His known work divides neatly into three periods. The earliest plays (through 425 B.C.) are *Archarnians, Knights, Clouds* and *Wasps*. In all of these he gave full rein to political satire. The second group (through 406 B.C.) are more reticent and cautious. They include *Birds, Lysistrata, Thesmophoriazusai* and *Frogs*. The last (through 388 B.C.) consist of *Ecclesiazusae* and *Plutus*, works that are "middle comedy" and contain no political allusions at all.

VALERIUS BABRIUS (second century A.D.) Greek fabulist

Babrius was a Hellenized Italian who was born at the end of the first century A.D. and lived well into the second. He spent his adult life in Syria and worked as tutor to a "King Alexander," a Semite who surrounded himself with Syrian scholars. Hence Babrius knew more about Assyrian and Babylonian literature than most Greeks, and drew upon these sources, as well as the Greek prose collections of Aesop (especially the Demetrius collection) for his own fables. He produced approximately two hundred fables, published in two books, and was the first to put Aesopic fables in iambic verse. Babrius always wrote in Greek, but his style—particularly the peculiar use of the iambic— was shaped by Latin, which was probably his mother tongue.

DONALD BARTHELME (1931–   ) American novelist and short-story writer

Donald Barthelme was raised in Houston, where he worked for several years as a newspaper reporter. Since 1962, he has been living in New York City. His short stories are collected in *Come Back, Dr. Caligari* (1964), *Unspeakable Practices, Unnatural Acts* (1968), *City Life* (1970) and *Sadness* (1972). Barthelme has also written a novel, *Snow White*.

WILLIAM BLAKE (1757–1827) English poet, painter, engraver, mystic

An artist before he was a writer, William Blake was apprenticed to James Basaire, an engraver, in 1771, and his first work was as a maga- zine illustrator. When he started to write and publish his own books (beginning with *Poetical Sketches*, 1783) he never considered his writ- ing as an activity separated from his art. He illustrated all of his work, and would be horrified by the fact that the major twentieth-century critics of his poetry all but ignore the accompanying art.

Harold Bloom has said, "Blake is at once the great intellectual satirist and the fiercest apocalyptic among the Romantics." The range of his work, from *Songs of Innocence* to the prophetic books such as *Milton* and *Jerusalem*, gives evidence to this.

JAMES BOSWELL (1740–1795) Scottish man of letters and biographer

Best known as diarist and biographer of Dr. Samuel Johnson, James Boswell was trained as a lawyer in Scotland, where he practiced for twenty years. He first met Dr. Johnson in 1763 and from then on visited him yearly in London until 1786, when he himself moved there permanently. Boswell spent the rest of his life "chronicling." *An Ac- count of Corsica* appeared in 1768 and the famous *Life of Samuel Johnson* in 1791. It has been said of the relationship between the two men that "Johnson owes much to Boswell, but it was Johnson who gave us Boswell." But the work published in Boswell's lifetime is only a fraction of what he wrote: the discovery of the Boswell Papers in the 1920's yielded approximately thirty volumes of material. He was not a great stylist but was an excellent journalist. The word "Boswell-ize" has been coined after him, meaning not just to record, but to get under the skin of one's subject matter.

CONSTANTINE P. CAVAFY (1863–1933) Greek poet

C. P. Cavafy was born in Alexandria into an upper-middle-class family that originally came from Constantinople. Although he himself became a Greek citizen and cultivated a love for that country which is reflected in his work, he spent most of his life in Alexandria—a city which he also loved and clearly needed for the development of his sensibility. He was uncommonly judicious about the publication of his poetry, throw-ing away a great percentage of what he wrote. And "publication" for Cavafy consisted of having pamphlets privately printed to be distributed among friends. It was not until two years after his death that the first public edition of his work appeared.

WILLIAM CAXTON (1422?–1491) English printer and translator

William Caxton came from a family of clothmakers and was expected to carry on the family tradition. He was apprenticed in England and in 1441 went to Bruges to complete his training. There he set up his own company and remained in the Low Countries for thirty years. In 1469 he began to translate and write while serving as the commercial advisor to the Duchess of Burgundy; but it was in 1471, when he went to Cologne and saw a printing press for the first time, that his second and more notable career was launched.

Caxton immediately learned how to use the press, returned to Bruges and set up his own. *Recuell* was the first book off the press: the first book ever to be printed in the English language. In 1476 Caxton returned to England and set up his shop in the precincts of West-minster Abbey. He edited all the books he printed and translated a third of them, usually from French or Latin; the two works best known today, *Reynard the Fox* and *Aesop*, were translated from the Dutch. Caxton's work was not very literal, but his quiet sense of humor and fine mastery of idiomatic prose served him well in his renditions of Aesop. They are still the most delightful retellings of those classical fables we have in the English language.

CHUANG TZU (369?–286? B.C.) Chinese Taoist philosopher

"All we know about the identity of Chuang Tzu, or Master Chuang, are the few facts recorded in the brief notice given him in the *Records of the Historian* by Ssu-ma Ch'ien (145?–89? B.C.). According to this account, his personal name was Chou, he was a native of a place called Meng, and he once served as 'an official in the lacquer garden' in Meng. Ssu-ma Ch'ien adds that he lived at the same time as King Hui (370–319 B.C.) of Liang and King Hsuan (319–301 B.C.) of Ch'i, which would make him a contemporary of Mencius, and that he wrote a work in 100,000 words or more which is 'mostly in the nature of Fable.'"

—from Burton Watson's introduction
to *The Complete Works of Chuang Tzu*

MARVIN COHEN (1929?–   ) American fiction writer

Marvin Cohen, a born New Yorker, lives on the Lower East Side and will leave that part of town only for yearly excursions to London. He has published two books, *The Self-Devoted Friend* (1968) and *The Monday Rhetoric of the Lame Club and Other Parables*. He teaches a workshop in creative writing.

JULIO CORTÁZAR (1914–   ) Argentine writer

Julio Cortázar was born in Brussels but spent the first part of his life in Argentina. In 1952 he moved to Paris and has been living there ever since. One of the finest writers in the Spanish language today, he is a master of literary forms, ranging from the novel to short pieces that might be considered prose poems. Among his works are *Hopscotch* (1965), *Cronopios and Famas* (1969) and *All Fires the Fire and Other Stories* (1973).

LEONARDO DA VINCI (1452–1519) Italian artist, scientist, writer

The notebooks of Leonardo are among the most interesting written documents left by a great visual and plastic artist. His style is one of extreme power and precision, recreating in poetic prose both the concepts and images that are present in his artistic work and in his scientific inventions. Mirror written, they were not properly deciphered and edited until the nineteenth century.

MARIE DE FRANCE (1160–1190) French poet

The half-sister of Henry II, Marie de France was born in Normandy, but spent most of her life at the English court. She is the author of two works, *Lais* and *Little Fables*. The former consists of fourteen romantic narratives in octosyllabic verse, the content based on Celtic legend. This work subsequently had a great influence on French writing.

JOHN DRYDEN (1631–1700) English poet, dramatist, critic

After his education at Trinity College, Cambridge, John Dryden moved on to London, where he made his living as a writer and wielded power over the intellectuals of his time (as Dr. Johnson did after him). In 1667 he was retained as writer to the king's theater and not long after served as poet laureate to Charles II. His satires aimed at Monmouth and Shaftesbury were written at the instigation of Charles. When James II came to the throne, Dryden converted to Catholicism—an act which, peculiarly enough, appears to have been genuine. Protection at court continued, and ceased only with the accession of William and Mary (for he did not revert back to Protestantism). At age sixty, Dryden was reduced once again to writing for the stage. *Absalom and Achitophel* (1681) is regarded as the greatest satire in the English language. Among his nonsatirical poetry are *The Hind and the Panther* and *A Song for Saint Cecilia's Day* (both 1687). As for his reworking of Chaucer, Dryden remarked that he simply "scrubbed up" the great poet!

JOHN GAY (1685–1732) English dramatist and poet

The son of an impoverished Devonshire family, John Gay lived the early part of his life on the bohemian fringes of the English literary world. He was first published in 1712, and in 1714 became a close friend of both Pope and Swift. From that period until his sudden death at forty-seven of an "inflammatory fever," Gay lived with a series of patrons as half guest, half retainer. He has been described as a lazy but gentle parasite—a fact to which he readily confessed when he wrote "while there's life, there's hope." His three most important works are *Trivia* (1716), *The Beggar's Opera* (1728) and *Fables in Verse* (1727–28).

HAN FEI TZU (——?–253 B.C.) Chinese Legalist scholar

A prince of the Han state, Fei Tzu was well and variously educated by the time he went off to study under the Confucian Hsün Tzu. He was enraged by the corruption of Han in its decline, and much of his writing was by way of admonishment. His works ultimately spread to the enemy Ch'n state, where they greatly impressed its king. He summoned Fei Tzu and took him into service. But the fact that he was a prince of Han provided ammunition for jealous courtiers. Eventually the king was persuaded that he might be harboring a spy and he jailed Fei Tzu. Only after he had been coerced into suicide did the king repent. Among the writings he left behind are *Solitary Indignation, Five Vermin,* and *The Difference in the Way of Persuasion.*

JOHANN GOTTFRIED von HERDER (1744–1803) German critic, author, and divine

Born in East Prussia, Herder studied theology at the University of Königsberg. There he formed friendships with people who were to have considerable influence on his thinking, including Kant. In 1767, expanding on Lessing's thesis, he attacked German hero-worship of other languages, rejecting "unhistorical imitation" in creating and evaluating literature. He later extended this theme into a renunciation of rationalism in art, and the conviction that cultural history must be reevaluated in terms of primitivism, spontaneity and originality. Herder evolved as the dominant influence on German romanticism and the theorist of the "Storm and Stress" movement. He spent his life as a preacher, educator, and writer, although he considered himself a teacher above all. He has come down to us as one of the great prose writers of German literary history. Among his works are *Outlines of a Philosophy of the History of Man* (1784–94), *God: Some Conversations* (1787), and a rather lyrical collection of fables.

HESIOD (eighth century B.C.) Greek poet

Hesiod was the son of a poor fisherman and lived most of his life as a farmer in Boeotia. His *Works and Days* was apparently addressed to a brother who cheated Hesiod of much of his share in family property. That work is a recounting of daily life in the fields, intermingled with fables and allegories. His other work that has come down to us is *Theogony*, which describes the beginnings of the world and the birth of the gods. He is known as "the father of Greek didactic poetry."

HORACE (Quintus Horatius Flaccus) (68–8 B.C.) Roman poet and satirist

The son of a freedman, Horace was born in Lucania and educated in Rome and Athens. In 42 B.C. he commanded a legion in the republican party at Philippi. The rest of his life he was comfortably patroned. Maecenas gave him a villa in the Sabine Hills, and he was a favorite of Emperor Augustus. His works consist of two books of satire, one of epodes, four of odes, two of epistles, and the *Ars Poetica*.

HSÜN TZU (second century B.C.) Chinese Confucian scholar

What little is known of Hsün Tzu is pieced together from his own works and a brief biography written a century after his death. He was born circa 312 B.C. in the state of Chao in central northern China. At the age of fifty he was invited to the court of Ch'i, during the time when the rulers of this new dynasty encouraged the patronage of scholars by way of proving its grandeur. But Hsün Tzu soon became the object of "slanderous talk" and he fled to Ch'u, where he was appointed magistrate of the Lan-Ling region in Shantung. He lived there until his death.

He led a long and quiet life that was given over primarily to teaching and study, with only minor excursions into local politics. Like Confucius and Mencius before him, his impact was not felt in his lifetime, and he died in relative obscurity. Hsün Tzu's thinking produced the most complex and well-ordered philosophical system in early Chinese history, and his literary style was second only to that of Chuang Tzu. It is ironic, however, that such a great Confucian should produce as his most famous disciple the Legalist Han Fei Tzu.

TED HUGHES (1930–   ) English poet

Ted Hughes served in the RAF as a ground wireless operator in East Yorkshire, where he had "nothing to do but read and re-read Shakespeare and watch the grass grow." He then entered Cambridge University, from which he was graduated in 1954. Aside from a two-year stay in the United States, he has lived in the English countryside. He is the author of four books for children, one play, and four collections of poetry, the latest of which is *Crow*.

LEONARD JENKIN (1940–   ) American writer

Leonard Jenkin was born in New York City and received his doctorate in English Literature from Columbia University. He now teaches at Manhattan Community College in New York.

JAMES JOYCE (1882–1941) Irish novelist

James Joyce was born near Dublin, during the era of hope in Parnell. During his early teens he wrote prize-winning essays; one, titled "My Favorite Hero," was on Ulysses. He was a brilliant student of languages, but would not touch Gaelic, a fact which speaks about his ambivalent attitude toward Ireland. In 1901 he denounced the proposed public theater as being a betrayal of the artist, who should know no national boundaries. Joyce left for Paris after graduating from University College, Dublin, but was called back to Ireland because his mother was dying. He taught at the Clifton School, Dalkey (an experience that later made its way into *Ulysses*). In 1904 he married and left Ireland permanently. The next twenty-five years of his life were spent first in Trieste and later in Paris. They are marked by one long history to get published and a fight against censorship. *The Dubliners* was completed in 1904 but was not published until 1914. In 1912 Joyce went back to Ireland to buy back the rights to *The Dubliners*, which was under contract there. Not only did the printer refuse to sell the sheets, he destroyed the type. Joyce resolved never to return to Ireland again. *Portrait of the Artist As a Young Man* was begun in 1904 and received its first publication in book form in America in 1916. *Ulysses* (begun in 1914) was privately published by Sylvia Beach in Paris, 1922, but was not legally published until 1933 in America by Random House. *Finnegans Wake*, which took Joyce seventeen years to write, appeared in 1939. Joyce died before its greatness was properly recognized. The American scholar Harry Levine was one of that work's first admirers and wrote of it: "The detachment which can look upon the conflicts of civilization with so many competing vocables is wonderful and terrifying."

FRANZ KAFKA (1883–1924) Czech-Austrian writer

Kafka was born in Prague, of a wealthy Czech-Jewish family. His writing career began at twenty-three when he entered a story in a contest sponsored by the Viennese periodical *Zeit*. In 1908 he was appointed to a semi-governmental post which permitted him the time to study Czech and write. At about this time he began to suffer from severe headaches and frayed nerves—a condition which drove him to the mysticism of the cabala. This, together with the sense of fatality he found underlying the works of Kierkegaard and Pascal, was to become a lasting influence on his life and writing. *Observations*, his first book, was published in 1912. Subsequently he wrote the first chapter of *Amerika* and worked on *Metamorphosis*. In 1913 he finished *The Judgement*, dedicated to a woman whom he had loved tragically for five years. This work, and a few stories, were all that were published in his lifetime. He grew increasingly ill and died in a sanitarium in Kosterneuberg. Kafka instructed his publisher to burn his manuscripts on his death, but this was not done, and *The Castle*, *The Great Wall of China*, *The Trial* and *Amerika* were all published posthumously.

IVAN IVANOVICH KHEMMITSER (1745–1784) Russian fabulist

A Russian of German émigré parents, Ivan Khemmitser was born in the district of Astrakhan. He served in the army until he was twenty-five, when he retired to accept a modest post as translator, and began his literary career. Like many other fabulists, he wrote overt and pungent satire before turning to the fable form. It is exclusively for the latter that he is remembered as a writer, and is thought to be the finest fabulist in Russia before Krylov. The first edition of Khemmitser's fables consisted of twenty-seven pieces and was published anonymously in 1779. A second edition of thirty-six fables appeared in 1782—also anonymously. That same year he died in Smyrna, where he was the Russian consul general. His fables are rich in social detail and in dialogue and—unprecedented in the Russian tradition of fable writing —omit a concluding moral.

COUNT IGNACY KRASICKI (1735–1801) Polish poet, novelist, playwright

Ignacy Krasicki was born in Polish Ruthenia and spent the first part of his life as a successful politician. Around 1774 he gave up politics to write, producing first satirical sketches and later poetry, fiction and fables. He was much influenced by Swift and Rousseau, and his best work is addressed to comic descriptions of the habits, customs and vices of the Polish community. As a fabulist he did not strive to imitate La Fontaine's poetic grace, but perfected the technique of compact and precise storytelling. Among his other works are *The Fashionable Wife* and *Drunkenness*.

IVAN ANDREVICH KRYLOV (1768–1844) Russian fabulist

Ivan Krylov was born in Moscow. Because his father died when he was eight, he was forced to interrupt his education and at fourteen went to work as a clerk in St. Petersburg. His early contact with "the people of the streets" was later to have a strong influence on his fables, which are mostly original, and sharply critical of both the Russian intelligentsia and the government. Krylov's first works were unsuccessful comic operas, but soon thereafter he began writing satire. From 1793 to 1803 he edited *The Spectator* and *The St. Petersburg Mercury*, until his editorial activities were suppressed, and he "disappeared" for the next ten years. In 1805 he reemerged and translated some fables by La Fontaine. They were enthusiastically received; with the encouragement of the fabulist Dimitrieu, Krylov chose that mode for his own work. These, too, were an immediate success and in 1812 he was offered a post in the St. Petersburg library, which he held for the next thirty years. Of all the major fabulists, Krylov is the most original. He invented all but a few fables he wrote, usually inspired by common or "journalistic" events. He was extremely nationalistic in tone and his style was linked with the eighteenth century. He did not assimilate new trends. Rather his skill involved a fusion of classical mannerisms and Russian colloquial language.

JEAN DE LA FONTAINE (1621–1695) French poet and fabulist

La Fontaine was brought up in Château-Thierry, the son of the "master of waters and forests" of that region. His early attentiveness to animal behavior, which the knowledge of the hunt requires, informed some of the fables he was later to write. As a young man he was restless, lacking a sense of purpose or enthusiasm of any kind. He spent eighteen months studying for the clergy but gave that up, and from 1646 to 1647 studied law as a pretext for trips to Paris. He inherited his father's job, which gave him time to write and provided a base in the country. But he was as unattentive to that as to all his other endeavors, including his marriage. From 1656 to 1661 La Fontaine was under the patronage of Fouquet, which ended abruptly when Louis XIV instigated the latter's downfall. He finally published his first important work, the bawdy *Contes*, in 1665. It created a censorial stir among the conventional members of Parisian intelligentsia. La Fontaine fared much better than Fouquet. He spent the remainder of his life (with the exception of ten "lean" years) in Paris, supported by a series of distinguished patrons. The first collection of fables (books one to six) was published in 1668; the second (books seven to eleven) in 1678; in 1694 he completed his opus with the publication of book twelve. These also were met with controversy. Like Phaedrus before him, he had to defend his work against the theorists of the day who argued that the fable myth of man as animal was essentially prosaic, and that to elevate such subject matter to the level of poetry was to deny the essential quality of poetry. La Fontaine replied that the fable and the epic fused two fundamental human mythologies, or "lies": the fiction of man the demigod and the fiction of man the animal. The fables delighted the salons where he recounted them, and despite these formalistic controversies, he was elected to the French Academy in 1684. Three years before his death, La Fontaine suffered from a near-fatal illness which induced him to repent his licentious *Contes* and equally libertine life-style, and he lived out those years in severe austerity.

THOMAS EDWARD LAWRENCE (1888–1935) English

Known as a writer on the basis of his one extraordinary book, *The Seven Pillars of Wisdom*, T. E. Lawrence was born in North Wales and at a very early age showed an interest in archeology. From 1910 to 1914 he studied Arabic in Syria, traveled through Northern Mesopotamia, and worked in Egypt. After two years as a staff captain with the British Intelligence department in Egypt, he went to Feisal, where he adopted Arab dress and organized diverse Arab tribes to fight against the Turks. After the war he was made a fellow at All Souls College, Oxford, and later, political advisor to the War Officer on Middle Eastern Affairs. During this time he completed four revisions of *The Seven Pillars of Wisdom*, which he finally published in a limited edition in 1926. Discouraged by the unfair treatment accorded the Arabs, and innately loathing the honors and power available to him (he turned down a knighthood and the Victoria Cross) he enlisted in the RAF as a common soldier under a pseudonym. He was discharged in 1935 and retired to Dorsetshire. Shortly afterward he was killed in a motorcycle accident. The fable included here was found among his private papers.

JOHN LENNON (1940–1980) English singer and writer

John Lennon, actor, author and **Beatle**, was born in Liverpool, and attended the Liverpool College of Arts. He has written two books of Liverpudlian nonsense poems and stories with his own illustrations, *In His Own Write* (1964) and *A Spaniard in the Works* (1965).

GOTTHOLD EPHRAIM LESSING (1729–1781)

Lessing was born in Saxony and educated at the University of Leipzig. Between 1749 and 1775 he lived in Berlin and produced two major works. The first was a collection of essays defending writers "misjudged" by previous generations. In it he asserted that the future of German drama lay in the imitation of English writing and rejected the French influence that he claimed had stultified German sensibility. The other was the domestic tragedy *Miss Sarah Sampson*. It was the first play written in Germany to break with the French tradition by using prose instead of Alexandrine verse and marked the beginning of modern German drama. In 1759, Lessing published a highly original collection of fables, which reveal an antagonism toward La Fontaine as much as a deep concern for the fable as a distinct form. He demonstrated this in the long preface to the collection, which is one of his finest pieces of criticism and remains the most thorough didactic work ever written on the fable. His greatest play, *Minna von Barnheim* (1767), was the first German national drama to be written. Lessing is regarded as the foremost representative of the intellectual ideals of the German Enlightenment.

SIR ROGER L'ESTRANGE (1616–1704) English journalist and political pamphleteer

Roger L'Estrange may or may not have attended Cambridge University and certainly had no profession until the Civil War, during which he was a convinced Loyalist and was imprisoned for espionage. The war provoked him into a career of political journalism. The course of his life can best be described as a continuous falling in and out of favor with the government as regimes changed. In 1663 he reached a pinnacle of power when Charles II appointed him "licenser of the press and surveyor of the imprimeries"—a long title that amounts to supreme censor of the press. L'Estrange wielded his power with a severity that condemned at least one man to death. He successfully published two magazines, the *Intelligencer* and the *News*, only to have them driven out by Henry Muddiman's *Gazette*. He gained, lost, and regained a seat in Parliament. From 1681 to 1687 he founded and ran the *Observer*, which James II was eventually obliged to repress, despite his personal sympathies with L'Estrange's views. The advantages of the knighthood bestowed upon him in 1685 counted for very little when he was imprisoned during the revolution of 1688. Of his three children, one died, a second was an invalid, a third became a Roman Catholic. In terms of the mores of those days, it is difficult to know which fate was the worst. L'Estrange died an impoverished bookseller's hack. The principal works of his later years were translations, the most famous being an edition of Aesop. To these fine renditions he appended his tiresome *Reflections*. They are amusing only in their dogmatism and so have been excluded from this collection.

PABLO NERUDA (1904–1973) Chilean Poet and diplomat

Pablo Neruda began publishing volumes of poetry in 1923, while still a student in Santiago. He spent much of the following fifteen years of his life abroad, as Consul for Chile in Rangoon, Colombo, Batavia, Singapore, Buenos Aires, Barcelona, Madrid, Paris and Mexico. He returned to Chile in 1943 via Machu Picchu in Peru, the subject of one of his most famous poems. In 1945 he joined the Communist party of Chile and was elected to the senate on its slate. His *Tercera* was published in 1947. Neruda was prosecuted for his Communism and went underground in 1948, beginning a long series of travels which took him to Russia and China. In 1950 his *Canto General* was published in Mexico, and he shared the World Peace Prize with Paul Robeson and Pablo Picasso in Moscow. He returned to Chile in 1952 and was awarded the Stalin Prize the following year. In 1970 he became Chile's ambassador in Paris, and in 1972 was awarded the Nobel Prize for Literature. He is once again resident in Chile.

THE PANCHATANTRA   Indian

The authorship of The Panchatantra is unknown, and its date of origin extremely vague. It was definitely in existence by 500 A.D., since in the sixth century it had been translated from the original Sanskrit into Pahlavi. Guesswork on the part of scholars places its origin somewhere between 100 B.C. and 500 A.D.

The various editions and translations have remained remarkably faithful to it. The original work was a book of stories and fables consisting of five sections and a brief introduction. Each of the five sections forms a dramatic unit in itself, and all five are set within the introduction as a frame. Each book contains a primary story (serving as a frame within *the* frame) and one or several "emboxed" stories— that is, stories represented as told by one character in the section-frame story to another. As in the body of Aesopian fables, the majority of the Panchatantra stories are peopled by animals with human attributes; others have only human characters and some, both people and animals. The pragmatic Machiavellian aspect of these tales is also similar to that in the European fable. One mistaken idea argues a relationship between The Panchatantra and Aesop. However, there is virtually no connection. Only two tales in The Panchatantra correspond with Aesop: "The Ass in Panther's Skin" and "The Ass Without Heart or Ears" (the latter is found in Babrius).

PHAEDRUS (circa 18 B.C.–circa 55 A.D.) Greco-Roman

All that we know about the life of Phaedrus has been gleaned from the confessional prologues to his five books of fables. He tells us that he was a Roman of lowly origin and was born on Pierian Mountain, "birthplace of the muses." As a boy he was a personal servant to Emperor Augustus and was educated with his grandsons, affording Phaedrus a fine classical training. Augustus ultimately freed him, and he began a stormy career as a fabulist. His first books were so controversial that, in 30 A.D., he was publicly condemned by the stern prosecutor and confidant of Tiberius, Aelius Sejanus. He was also attacked by critics for the assumption that his fables qualified as poetry, and it wasn't until the time of Avianus (circa 400 A.D.) that his work was justly recognized. All told, Phaedrus wrote a hundred fifty fables. As with Babrius, his main source was the prose collection of Aesop. However, he invented many fables of his own, and his work contains more originality and emphasis on fictional entertainment than is found in Babrius, even though the latter is generally considered to be a finer poet.

THEODORE ROETHKE (1908–1963) American poet

Theodore Roethke was born in Michigan and educated at University of Michigan and at Harvard. For most of his adult life he taught English at the University of Washington while writing poetry. Recognition came to him after the publication of his second volume, *The Lost Son* (1949). *The Waking* (1953) won the Pulitzer Prize; *Words for the Wind* came out in 1957, and *The Far Field* was published posthumously in 1965.

WILLIAM SAROYAN (1908–1981) American writer

William Saroyan was born in Fresno, California, of Armenian parents. He left school while in his teens, and worked for several years at odd jobs. In 1934 he published *The Daring Young Man on the Flying Trapeze*, which immediately launched his career as a writer. During the mid-thirties, he worked briefly in Hollywood and, by 1940, with *The Time of Your Life*, established himself as a playwright as well. Since then, he has written in almost every genre. His *Fables* (published in a limited edition in 1941) are all based on Armenian folklore.

WILLIAM SHAKESPEARE (1564–1616)

English dramatist and poet who, despite being the author of "insignificant and immoral works" (Tolstoy), "lacking the least spark of good taste and the slightest knowledge of rules" (Voltaire), and a fellow who (according to the first English drama critic, Thomas Ryner) "raves and rambles without any coherence," managed to do quite well for himself. Some claim that his works were written by Francis Bacon, or by "Divers of Worship" who could not allow their aristocratic names to be associated with the vulgar playhouse. But current opinion agrees that they come from the pen of William Shakespeare, or another chap of the same name.

CHRISTOPHER SMART (1722–1771) English poet

Christopher Smart's brilliant life as a scholar and poet was punctuated by bouts of alcoholism and madness. He was made a fellow of Pembroke College, Cambridge, in 1747 but lost the position because of his drinking and the debts he had incurred. He spent the year 1750 in the Bedlam asylum. When he was released he married and returned to Cambridge, forgiven. He won the Seatonian Prize for poetry and, as long as he kept on competing for it, and winning, Cambridge would keep him on. This he managed to do for several years. In 1775 he moved to London permanently and worked as a bookseller's hack for John Newberry, using the pseudonyms Ebenezer Pentweazle and Mary Midnight. His more serious writing included translations from Horace, but all this brought him little money, and finally his wife and daughter went to live with relatives in Ireland; Smart never saw them again. In 1763 he was back in Bedlam again, where he wrote his only first-rate poem, *A Song to David* (1763). His insanity took the form of religious mania and—according to the doctors—a lack of concern for "clean linnen." How insane he was is open to question: when Dr. Johnson visited him he remarked that he would "as lief pray with Kit Smart as with anyone" and that as for a lack of interest in clean linnen, the doctor "had no passion for that himself." Smart was released but remained an incurable alcoholic and died in the debtors' prison. His *Poetical Translation of the Fables of Phaedrus* was written in 1765.

EDMUND SPENSER (1552?–1599) English poet

Edmund Spenser was educated at Pembroke Hall, Cambridge, where he was deeply influenced by the mixture of neo-Platonic and Calvinistic thinking which characterized that college. By 1578, when he was already well at work on *The Faerie Queene*, he was appointed Deputy of Ireland and unwillingly spent most of his life there. His occasional brief returns to England were made to oversee the publication of that work and to seek a post at the court of Elizabeth I. All he ever received was an annual pension of fifty pounds. In 1597 his Kilcoman Castle was burned to the ground by the Irish, and he returned to England ill and penniless. He died shortly after he arrived. In his writing, he reconciled feudalism and the Renaissance; Christianity and paganism. But his greatest gift as a writer was his sense of language. He revived alliteration from early English verse after it had been superseded by rhyme, and combined the two in his work. He also invented the famed Spenserian stanza.

WALLACE STEVENS (1879–1955) American poet

Wallace Stevens was born in Reading, Pa., and educated at Harvard University and the New York University Law School. He practiced law from 1904 to 1916; then he joined the Hartford Accident and Indemnity Company, where he worked until his death. His poetry was first published in a 1914 issue of *Poetry*, edited by Harriet Monroe. His work was published and anthologized regularly after that, but because he was cautious about bringing out a volume of poetry, his first book, *Harmonium*, did not appear until 1923. This was followed by *Ideas of Order* (1936), *Owl's Clown* (1936), *The Man with the Blue*

Guitar (1937) and *Parts of a World* (1942). Delmore Schwartz has written of his work: "We are presented almost always with the poet, or the protagonist of the poem, in isolation before the tableau of Nature and Society, meditating upon them."

ROBERT LOUIS STEVENSON (1850–1894) Scottish novelist, poet, essayist

Robert Louis Stevenson was a man who was tubercular all his life and, perversely or logically, spent much of his life traveling hard and wide. He studied for the bar but never entered practice. Instead, he went to Europe, which resulted in the writing of *An Inland Voyage* (1878) and an encounter with an American woman whom he followed back to the United States and married in 1880. The following year he started writing prolifically and most successfully. In 1883 he published *Treasure Island*, which made him a fortune. Following hard upon that was *A Child's Garden of Verse* (1885), *The Strange Case of Dr. Jekyll and Mr. Hyde* and *Kidnapped* (1886). By 1887 his health was seriously failing, and after moving from spa to spa in Europe he went to Saranac Lake in America, where he wrote *The Master of Ballantrae*. The Stevensons kept on moving, first to the West Coast then on to Samoa. There he spent the last five years of his life as a planter and acting "chief of the natives." Stevenson died suddenly of apoplexy shortly after completing *The Wrecker*.

JAMES THURBER (1894–1961) American writer and cartoonist

Born in Columbus, Ohio, James Thurber began his writing career as a newspaper reporter, first for the Columbus *Dispatch* and later for the Chicago *Tribune* in Paris. He joined the staff of *The New Yorker* in 1926 and wrote for "The Talk of the Town." In 1933 he left *The New Yorker*, but for the rest of his life published his stories, satires, fables and cartoons there so regularly that, along with E. B. White, he is said to have established the tone of that magazine. Through his work, he perfected a form of humor which, T. S. Eliot remarked, "is also a way of saying something serious." Thurber is the only twentieth-century writer to write an opus of fables, which are collected in two volumes, *Fables For Our Time* and *Further Fables For Our Time*. Among his many other publications are *My Life and Hard Times* (1933), *Men, Women and Dogs* (1943) and *Thurber Country* (1953).

COUNT LEO NIKOLAYEVICH TOLSTOY (1828–1910) Russian novelist and moralist

Leo Tolstoy was born on the family estate at Yasnaya Polyana, a hundred miles south of Moscow. In the first half of his life he was as dissolute, restless, and without focus as he was productive, dogmatic and conservative throughout the second part of his life. Tolstoy was a spoiled child, educated at home by German and French tutors. In 1844 he went to Kazan University to study Oriental languages but was thrown out for laziness. He obstinately refused to meet women of society, preferring those of the streets. In 1851 he returned to Yasnaya Polyana, which he had by then inherited, only to find himself bored with the country. So he took off with his brother to the Caucasus and joined the army as a cadet. It was at this time that he began writing. *Childhood* was published in 1852 and gained him immediate critical attention. He fought in the Crimean war and recorded those experiences in *Sevastopol Sketches*. After the war he went to St. Petersburg, where Turgenev introduced him to the literary world. During the 1850's, Tolstoy became interested in education, and started an experimental school at Yasnaya Polyana in which grades were abolished as a motive for learning and spontaneity was encouraged. In 1862, the year that marks the major transition in his life, he married Sofya Andreyevna Bers, who in time bore him thirteen children. He settled into the life of a country landowner. The eighteen sixties and seventies proved to be his most productive period. *War and Peace* was written between 1862 and 1869, and *Anna Karenina*, between 1873 and 1876. As reflected in *Anna Karenina*, his own marriage was by then disintegrating. After 1878, Tolstoy gave up literary writing and turned to treatises such as *My Confession* and *What Is Art*, which reflect the moralist/philosopher/teacher he had become. In 1910 he fled the madness of his wife and died en route in the railway station of Astapol.

JOHN WEBSTER (1580?–1625?) English dramatist

Very little is known about John Webster. He probably received no formal education, but picked up scraps of classical learning from the better-educated playwrights with whom he associated. He wrote many plays, and collaborated with other writers on many more. The comedies were inevitably failures, but he had a greatness for tragedy. In a sense he is a great tragic poet more than a successful playwright—spiritually akin to Donne. *The White Devil* and *The Duchess of Malfi* are his two masterpieces.

SIR THOMAS WYATT (1503?–1542) English diplomat and poet

Thomas Wyatt was reared with Anne Boleyn and probably was her first lover. He was educated at John's College, Cambridge; not long after graduation he was sent on a mission to France. In 1536 he was abruptly thrown into London Tower with Anne Boleyn, but since he was held there for only a month, and knighted the following year, it is doubtful that their affair was suspected. From 1537 to 1540 Wyatt was ambassador to Spain, then to Flanders and Paris, from where he was suddenly recalled and unfairly imprisoned in the Tower a second time on a charge of treason. After his release, he retired to his birthplace in Kent and spent the rest of his life as Knight for the Shire of Kent.

Because of his primary interest in diplomacy, the opus of Wyatt's poetry is small, but the importance and beauty of his work cannot be overestimated. He was the first writer of the true English sonnet, which was modeled on the work of Petrarch. Surrey, a much younger man, was taught by Wyatt. It has been said that Wyatt "drew ideas out of Italy for the rejuvenation of English poetry." He also was the first English poet to introduce personal concerns into his work.

WILLIAM BUTLER YEATS (1865–1939) Irish poet and dramatist

William Butler Yeats's early childhood was divided between London and County Sligo, Ireland, and the latter part of it was spent in Dublin. As a young adult he returned to London, where he became one of the *fin de siècle* poets. During this period he dabbled in various occults, and his mystical tendencies were in full play throughout his early work. In 1896 he returned to Ireland, where he was caught up in the rebellion and especially with its "queen," Maud Gonne. His work of this period is beautiful and soft—a little too soft. At a time when Yeats found himself totally without direction in both his writing and his life, Lady Gregory came to his rescue and involved him in the founding of the Abbey Theatre. His poetry grew more "immediate in its hold on reality"; it was the least mystical period of his work.

In 1917 Yeats married Georgie Lee, settled on the Irish coast, and became a member of the senate. Georgie Lee turned out to be a medium and reawakened the mystic in Yeats, which found its way into his latest work without overpowering it. Yeats won the Nobel Prize for Literature in 1923.

Index